DEFINING YOUR PURPOSEFUL PROSPERITY PATH

How to Make Opportunities, a Business Model, and a Living from Your Wisdom

Lynn M. Scheurell

FREE – Companion PDF

This book includes a FREE downloadable collection of key exercises you can use to help identify your Prosperity Path.

Get It NOW at
LynnScheurell.com/prosperity-exercises

MIZRAHI PRESS

Defining Your Purposeful Prosperity Path:
How to Make Opportunities, a Business Model
and a Living from Your Wisdom

ISBN-13: 978-0-9801550-7-5

Limit of Liability/Disclaimer of Warranty

While the author has used their best efforts in preparing this report, they make no representation or warranties with respect to the accuracy or completeness of the contents and specifically disclaim any implied warranties. The advice and strategies contained herein may not be suitable for your situation. You should consult with a professional where appropriate. The author shall not be liable for any loss of profit or any other commercial damages, including but not limited to special, incidental, consequential or other damages.

Published by Mizrahi Press
A Division of Creative Catalyst LLC
MyCreativeCatalyst.com

Table of Contents

Author's Note

I've lived the best of times and the worst of times over the years through my business. My intention is to give you what I wish I had known along the way so you can save time and energy and enjoy more of the best times through your business.

My friend named me as the Creative Catalyst when I started my business in 1998. At the time, I was feeling trapped in a corporate career, having been a serial entrepreneur on the side for about 15 years by then. As I sat with my friend, I asked him to tell me what I did that was unique. What he shared seemed just too easy—and I was overlooking it. It didn't seem big or important enough to build a business from it because it came so naturally to me. (I did not know then that is one of the keys to your ideal prosperity path.)

Without hesitation, he said, "You're a Creative Catalyst. You make change happen." The power of that moniker just about knocked me over. It felt so right that, in that moment, everything changed. I couldn't go back to what had been—I needed to live into being a Creative Catalyst. Naturally, there were no rulebooks, and I didn't know any other catalysts, so I wasn't sure what to do next.

So I did what any reasonably self-aware person would do when they don't know what they're doing—I tried everything. I read books, went to seminars, and took classes. I modeled what other people were doing. I watched videos, took home-study programs, and went to live events. I networked, worked with guru-types, and searched my soul. The first few years of my business were as a Feng Shui practitioner solely because my business coach told me that's what I should focus on (vs. life coaching, which was my other option at the time).

I was busy studying energy and teaching people how to get their environment sorted out to support them in getting what they wanted while I was figuring out how to get my own business on track. As I worked with my clients, it was a privilege to see how their lives bloomed as a result of our work together. The first Feng Shui class I taught was to four people in the back of a little tiny retail shop; the second was in a commercial demo kitchen on the second floor of a grocery store. (One of the participants thought Feng Shui was a fancy mushroom.)

I was learning business growth strategy by doing it. At some point, I thought I might as well get some return on my investment in the business-building classes I was taking at the local chamber of commerce, and I wanted to help people. So I began teaching classes with one foot in the energy world and one foot in the business development world.

I would find myself in front of these groups of students, paying attention to their questions and challenges. I heard an inherent pain in how they were going about their businesses. They were in these classes to learn about what wasn't working and how to solve it. They wanted change but didn't know how to go about getting it. And they were focusing on tactics as the "magic wand" that would make it all better. But I knew there was something else that wasn't being considered yet.

When I went home after teaching, I would wonder what I was being shown so I could help these committed, driven, intelligent soul-driven business owners to move their businesses forward for positive results (and more joy). People started asking me to do personal sessions to get specific about addressing their challenges. Over time, while doing what I loved and helping people reach new levels of awareness, I came to understand there was a process each person went through to reach their answers.

It wasn't about using some new marketing tactic, nor was it about throwing money at advertising to get visibility. It was about being open to and accepting change based on accessing their own unique wisdom.

I also learned that I was more unique than I ever thought because it came easily to me. I thought everybody knew how to do what I did—that everyone knew how to handle change and make things happen. I assumed everybody else knew how to read energy too, and could then synthesize their insights into relevant clarity for informed decision-making. The reality is I had stumbled onto my prosperity path by which to share my wisdom.

Understand from Inside Out

To make a short story just a little bit longer, the shortcut I discovered was that when people understood their life purpose from the inside out, their business(es) would bloom because they started being in alignment with what mattered to them. They had words to describe what they always "kind of knew." And they chose the marketing strategies and tactics that reflected their authenticity versus just random fumbling around or doing it just because they saw someone else have success with it. And they would feel great. They would be excited about going into work and they saw their bigger contribution to the world around them. It was their bigger footprint, their ability to be more significant, and feel more fulfilled personally and professionally because they were stepping into and living from their true-life purpose.

This book is about that system in terms of knowing and trusting your wisdom, discovering your life purpose, and charting your prosperity path to earn a living from it. Chances are that it is much easier than you thought...and maybe harder to do until you have clarity.

Essentially, when you are questioning your life purpose, you're losing time and energy and opportunities because you're still searching for it instead of living from it. Your business is a reflection of you so it is matching your growth or your stuckness. It's matching your state of mind, your beliefs, and the results of the decisions you're making while you're preoccupied with that search for your life purpose. That's continuing to run in the back of your mind, even when you know you can access your wisdom to benefit others.

Remember, I know about that one personally because, back when I was still searching, my life was on life support as a result of being trapped in corporate jobs that were supporting my habit of entrepreneuring. That was all my friends thought—that I just had this bad 'habit' of entrepreneuring. When I finally tuned into my wisdom, combined with my purpose and prosperity path, to map out a system to help my clients step into their authentic essence in business, everything started clicking. So if you don't understand why you're focusing on what you do and why you aren't getting the results you think you should be getting, because you're going through the motions or following the herd, then it's about getting really intimate with your wisdom, life purpose, and prosperity path.

At this point in my business, some 20-odd years after my friend named me the Creative Catalyst, I've worked with thousands of business owners and helped them make hundreds of thousands of dollars. And it's been really interesting because I've attracted the attention of some big-name, guru-types along the way. Now, these people don't actually really ever talk about who they're working with, but I can tell you one of my clients has called me his "stealth weapon for business evolution." I love that. It's what I'm all about—personal transformation and business evolution, helping people to express who they are through their businesses.

One of the biggest mistakes I see is people staying in confusion or overwhelm as they're launching or growing their business because they don't know what to do next. Not only that, but we've entered the age of energy ... first business was centered on agriculture, then industry, then experience, now energy. This is a time where everything is different—the old ways just don't work anymore until we figure it out from the inside out and THEN apply various models of business and marketing.

The greater path is the interior path because, as you align with who you are, your external world manifests accordingly. It's no longer about security or setting up a business based on what the marketplace wants; rather, it's about expressing your unique purpose for your optimal prosperity.

You're in the Right Place if…

If you…

    … are driven to do your life's work as a business,

    … must leave your mark in the world by following your destiny,

    … make your unique contribution to the world through your personal gifts,

    … risk taking what's important to you and expressing the essence of it to create a business,

    … hear your calling and have no choice other than to follow it,

    … use your life, through your business, to be of service,

then you are the 'new' entrepreneur. That means that there is a new way of doing business that resonates with you around life purpose and delivering value in your own unique way.

If you're feeling pulled to do something more in your life and business, this book is a solid resource for you. If you know you can be happier every day, that you want to express and make your purpose manifest in the world through your business, you're going to gain insights by reading what's in these pages. You're in the right place if you have the courage to risk taking what's important to you and sharing it out there in the world. If you're ready to step into and claim the power of your soul's wisdom for greater connection, this book can help you. If you're looking to go beyond where you've been to live and act from what really matters to you, and you're ready to take action, this is definitely the right resource for you.

The Not-Knowing Feeling

As you learn, you will experience the 'not-knowing' feeling, which is a good thing. The confusion as your linear mind sorts out what you are just "knowing"—your intuition. It is the jumping off place from where you are to where you want to be. Your emotions are your body's way of processing thoughts, and are clues to shifts in consciousness. That's important information for a soul-driven entrepreneur.

People will say something like, "gosh, I just don't know what I'm supposed to be doing. I don't have the resources that I think I need. I don't have the money. If I could live my wisdom on purpose and walk my prosperity path to fame and fortune, that'd be great, but I have to be a millionaire already to do it." They are looking for reasons to prove themselves right in what they already know—which is that they don't believe they have a prosperity path or unique purpose or wisdom. They don't know how something can work so they negate it.

However, the not-knowing feeling is the jumping off place to your possibilities and to your intuition. It means you are open to fresh opportunities and seeing things in a new way—you are not locked into what you already know. The not-knowing feeling means getting more comfortable with uncertainty and even ignorance, which allows more energy to move. There is not a constriction there prohibiting what you're willing to see, experience, and learn.

Growth is discomfort. If you're comfortable, you're not growing. So the not-knowing is growing beyond anything that you know, are familiar with, and expect—but it can also feel really destabilizing as you sort out what's next. The not-knowing feeling is actually the place of possibility. It means you are going beyond where you've already been. There's a magic in that, but the not-knowing feeling can be really destabilizing. That was part of the unique challenges you face in identifying your purpose. How can you feel centered when everything's in chaos? How do you maintain equilibrium when you don't know what's going to happen next or where you're going to get what you need to do your purpose next, whatever that is?

It can also be destabilizing because what if you discover you've been doing your purpose all along but didn't know it? That happens because your purpose is always trying to express itself. It's just that you may not have known that's what it was or you discounted it like my client did. The not-knowing feeling is actually the place to embrace your next level.

So keep that in mind the next time you think, "Oh gosh, I don't know how to do that. I don't know what to do instead of panicking." In that moment, you are in the place of possibility. And that is what helps set the stage for your prosperity path going forward.

Three Ways to Know You're Ready for Change

There are three ways to know you're ready for big change. First, you may find yourself having a sense of restlessness. I call it being a "Lamborghini trapped behind a lawnmower." You're restless, but you don't know quite where to go. Second, you might also notice things are ending such as relationships or opportunities. And third, new opportunities might be coming to you. These opportunities might be on the fringes of your awareness or more obvious. Any of these three experiences can signal that a shift is imminent.

Now, you might be thinking, "That's great . . . but I don't know what that means or what that looks like or how to do it." The not-knowing feeling you have is the confusion as your linear mind is sorting out what you know by your innate wisdom. In reality, it's the jumping off place from where you are to where you want to be—the place of possibility. Your emotions are your body's way of processing thoughts and their clues to shifts in consciousness. That's important information for anyone considering making a living from their wisdom. One of my clients described it as feeling like she was floating with no orientation in space. She was grabbing for the railing but, even if she could grab it, she didn't know if she, or it, was up or down or whatever. That's why we need to have that internal center through our wisdom to help balance us. Wisdom is an internal knowingness.

Making a living from your wisdom is a choice. It's not enough to know you have valuable wisdom—you must feel compelled to share it to help others *and* be paid for sharing it. When your wisdom calls you out to make a living from it, your life changes in profound and exponential ways.

Investing in your own growth is the best investment you can make toward being successful in your prosperity path. This is an issue for many wisdom workers who just want to help people. Making an investment in self is not a selfish pursuit; instead, it is selfless as you willingly step into your next best level for your own and everyone else's benefit. It's the best thing you can do to help other people because feeling like you are not enough or contributing value to others can lead to self-doubts and self-sabotage. By turning inward and doing the work to grow, you become the person on the inside who automatically expresses the outer authentic manifestation of your wisdom in business.

Enhancing your awareness of what's happening in your life is the most direct path to conscious freedom, fulfillment, and fun.

What to Expect from This Book

I'm not the ultimate expert; instead, I'm sharing what I've learned through my clients and my personal experience. I continue to be a student of 'wisdom work' as a business and, really, all things related to the human condition and our truly awesome potential. So there is a lot of substance here to take in as you read. This is not a prescription to follow but, instead, is about shifting your awareness.

Some of what you will learn includes:

- The context of wisdom work as a career path for prosperity

- How your life purpose informs, gives meaning to, and guides your prosperity path

- Five keys to gaining insight about what's happening in your life

- What it means to work from (or, conversely, avoid) your life wisdom

- The ways that fear, resistance, and doubt are messengers for next-level success

- Practicalities in charting your prosperity path through being a business owner

- Tools you can use to identify opportunities and release what gets in the way

- Why friends and family are not really your best resource for change

- The power that is yours to access on command to help you make informed decisions

This book should give you some language to understand what is happening as you navigate your next-level success. Ideally, you will see the challenges you could face as your energy seeks alignment for living through purpose to prosperity as well as how to interpret life events to your benefit as sources of insight and to attract more of what you want to experience. There is far more than can be summarized here, which is strategic. You may not know what you need to learn or what can help you in moving forward. So there is a LOT of information here, all of which is written to be useful and practical.

My intention is you have the opportunity to apply what we're talking about and then have a sense of self-discovery about your purpose. That may not happen with blinding clarity. If you've got some stuff in the way, it can be like clouds that block the sun, which is always shining just as your purpose is always available to you. When the clouds block the light, you might think the sun isn't there—but it is; just as your purpose is always there as a beacon for how to direct your life force energy every day. The goal is to remove the blocks and support you in learning more about yourself in a powerful way.

Keep in mind that you do not have to read this book sequentially (although you can); instead, check out the sections that have the greatest appeal to you in the moment and read those first. Take time to distill and then integrate what you just read to see how it resonates for you and decipher any intuitive messages you might receive as a result. In fact, pay attention to your dreams and synchronicities (where things happen as "coincidence") for the next nine days after you read something as it can take time to perceive messages.

I also recommend you take note of anything that feels like a right strategy, takeaway, or insight you can use as you read the book. My clients often share that they gain so much information that they need to 'unpack' it all after they've taken in what was presented.

In any case, I trust you will receive what you need to help you get to your next-best level for success. And I'd love to hear about it— please reach out and let me know. (I hesitate to put an email address in here as it could change over time; however, I am certain to have a website presence until the end of my days so you can find me when it's the right timing for you.)

Let's begin...

The Context
of Wisdom Work

We have entered an age like none known before...I call it The Energy Economy.

Scientists have long known that everything is made of energy; the rest of us have finally figured out that form follows energy. That is, something cannot manifest physically unless it existed first in energetic form.

Your thoughts are an energy form—one of the most powerful, in fact. Your intentions, interpretations of life's experiences, and emotional expression are energy forms. Your state of being and relationships and self-worth are energy forms. And all of it, with your attention, becomes wisdom.

For the first time in history, people with wisdom are not only respected more deeply than the average civilian but they are respected enough to be paid for their wisdom. Others recognize the value of leveraging life lessons based on wisdom rather than living them personally, allowing them to focus on the good stuff without experimenting and, potentially, becoming distracted or paying an unnecessary toll of time, energy, and resources.

If you are called to be a Wisdom Worker in this 'Energy Economy,' it's likely that:

- You seem to 'know' things before others do (IF they ever do).

- You feel compelled to share or even teach what you know.

- Your life has had (seemingly) more challenges than others in superficial comparison.

- You feel 'connected' in ways that others don't appear to be by their words or actions.

- You are a high communicator and, possibly, an adopter of digital ways to engage with people.

- You've had people tell you you're an 'old soul.'

- You try to blend in with others but still 'stick out' enough that people seek your counsel (in strange places—parks, parties, the gym, etc.).

- You've had strangers share details with you they've not even breathed to their best friend.

- You see life with metaphysical eyes—you know that "messages" and guidance surrounds us.

It is you who will help guide people to their evolution to reach their next best level. That individual growth will form our collective future.

So you can see we all (those people you know and those you have yet to meet) . . . we ALL need you to define your prosperity path so you can be abundant and, therefore, have more to share with the rest of us. As you impact one person at a time, you change their world, which changes the world of their friends and family, which changes the next person's world . . . in other words, you are creating the future by sharing your wisdom.

Challenges of Becoming a Wisdom Worker

As a wisdom worker, you will encounter some unique challenges in discovering and then living and working from your prosperity path. Here's the irony...just because you have wisdom doesn't mean you know how to make a living from it. Maybe you're not comfortable talking about yourself. Maybe you just want to put your head down and work. Maybe you're intimidated (or even afraid of!) the dreaded "SALES" you have to do to be in business.

It's hard to feel wise and purposeful when your business (and life) feels unstable, or you don't know what's coming next, or you don't have the resources—money, relationships, environment or anything else—you think you need in a given moment. It can seem unrealistic to craft a prosperity path based on what you know because it feels like you don't know enough. It can be challenging to turn who you are into a business owner. And it can also mean leaving some people behind as a result of your growth through the business development journey. And, since wisdom workers are generally highly intelligent, creative, and insightful renaissance souls, focus can be difficult because there's possibility in everything.

Another mindset barrier wisdom workers can encounter is thinking that what they want to build their business around is too easy for them to do. We are conditioned to think that if it's easy, it must not be valuable. Just today I had a client session where my client said, "Oh, I do all this stuff—I just thought everybody else did too." Or you might want to think that other people are already doing it so your wisdom won't be valuable—but nobody else knows exactly what you know or can communicate it in the same way.

By consciously living your wisdom, you are breaking the bonds of social context. A lot of people will choose to live and decide what's important to them based on other people's expectations, opinions, or guidance. To discover your prosperity path is to pursue conscious growth. In doing that, you can't un-ring a bell. You are now responsible for what you discover and how it applies and becomes a foundation for your life.

Once in business, you as a wisdom entrepreneur could encounter any of the following stumbling blocks that have the power to hold you back in business.

1. Too many ideas
2. Not knowing what to work on first—everything is a priority
3. Doing it all alone (vs. delegating)
4. Not knowing the value of your service, product, or time
5. Not knowing how to sell your services as a purveyor of transformation

At the same time, you're committed to sharing your wisdom because you know the difference it can make for others. You love serving people! And maybe you've even made some money at it but you know you can (and want/need) to make more. So you're committed to doing what it takes to follow your calling as a wisdom worker into becoming a business owner so you can get paid to share what you know.

The good news is it's actually not hard to do. In fact, once you understand the strategy of it and align with your unique purpose, you will see how you can progress your clients through greater levels of value in your work in a way that serves both of you.

If you are called to the entrepreneurial way, it's likely you've got what's called the 'bright shiny object syndrome.' Meaning, you want to do this, and this, and oh—there's that too! It can be overwhelming to try to round up all your knowledge, expertise, and talent to all focus in the same direction. But that's what needs to happen . . . the good news is you're ready to learn the truth about opportunities, your wisdom, your purpose, and how to present them in a viable, progressed business model as your path to prosperity.

The Stages of Knowing

Let's talk about the stages of knowing . . . as in, how do you know what you know to know whether something is really right for you? And what is the stage of knowing that potentially generates the most business?

There are three stages of knowing what you want, which can be interesting to explore. The first stage is not knowing you know or not knowing what you want. The second stage is knowing what you know or want but not knowing how to get or talk about it. This is the point marketers play on to get you to buy stuff because it can be really painful to know you don't know. And a lot of teaching comes from this angle, meaning that when you know you don't know but you want to learn, you can get the information you want and need—but if you didn't know you didn't know, then you wouldn't know a class, product, or service would have value to offer you. This is where you will find many of your clients and students as they struggle to learn what they know they want or need.

Finally, the third stage is knowing you know, which is ideal for going beyond and developing a new knowingness because you have to know what you know as a foundation for growth. This is where I find it common to be 'tested' for having or nearly having what you want, meaning that something will happen to challenge your new knowingness. For example, when you commit to a new exercise routine, you might find your schedule suddenly books up so you don't have time or you want to sleep in or your workout buddy cancels on you. This kind of test is not something you are graded on but, instead, gives you a way to see whether you practice / live what you now know. My theory is that, in the third stage, we get tested in multiples of three. In my metaphysical studies, I've learned that three is the number the universe runs on metaphysically. Some say deaths come in threes. Sneezes come in threes. And, in terms of tests about knowing what you want, they come from different angles.

All these stages can cause doubt about what you want but, in the end, you're actually stronger by going through them.

How this relates to your purposeful prosperity path is that, at first, you don't really know where you're at or what's happening. Then you get a sense of where you think you're supposed to be but don't know how to be in that, what you're supposed to do or what the rules are for being in that place. This comes up often for business owners and entrepreneurs because they're always trying, or being forced to accommodate, new things. The third test happens when you can't believe you're in this situation, relationship, or business and it's not doing what you want (meaning, it's not producing as expected).

For example, an entrepreneur wants more cash flow so s/he tries a new revenue model. S/he isn't sure how to market it but tries something anyway. S/he talks with other people, looks for models they can emulate . . . then s/he does this uncomfortable thing with the expectation that it will work as it has in the past or like it does for other people. At that point, there is a realization it's really not working to get enough clients. Each step is a learning journey. Each step is a progression toward you becoming stronger, better and clearer about doing what you do with purposeful wisdom. It's an active process that comes up with different circumstances and, while potentially frustrating, is always rewarding in the end.

Sometimes we might not know if we're being tested or if the universe is sending signals we misread or if we should be going in an entirely different direction with what we want or are doing. If we apply the Law of Attraction, are we actually having, being or doing something without being aware of it? Or are we reading the scenario, seeing what's coming and then preparing for it? Are you being tested for something because you're actually doing it or are you being blocked because you shouldn't go that direction?

If something is unreasonably hard or isn't flowing, either there's another way or there's something missing or there's a block. There is a difference between a test and being blocked. When you're blocked, you're really stuck because the universe is protecting you in some way. You can, of course, push through that but it could be disastrous. It's better to stop and 'read' the situation for various options.

Personally, when I get blocked, I stop and check in to see what I might be missing. It might be that I'm being blocked because I didn't quite finish my current opportunity yet and need to do something further or more complex than I knew or that I thought I did but didn't. It's almost like a little gateway before I can move forward.

As an example, one of my clients got an insight that she needed to take some downtime in December. At the time, she was teaching dance at two different locations, so she was going to speak with them both about her intention to take a few weeks off. Part of her reasoning was that the class numbers were really low in both places. On the days when she was going to talk to the owners, her class was completely full. She had a third person she was going to ask to cover her class; her plan was to call the next evening to ask for coverage. The day before she called, that person proactively called her to say the newspaper was going to be there during her class to produce a news article. So was that a block or a test? Did she miss the message or get a sign?

Those are the moments that can rock us back on our heels. It's important to pay attention and put both energy and focus toward the high payoff activities, to relax into what feels right, to ignore the busy work and not get sucked into all the potential distraction. There are times when the best thing you can do is just wait to get clarity. You can ask if "this" is something to move forward with at this time with what I have to work with, then wait to see how it feels. If it's dark, heavy, sludgy, or doesn't feel good, that's a no. If you get a no, ask further questions—is that a no for right now or for forever?

Some say there is a fourth stage, which is knowing but not knowing because you're living it as second nature and with mastery. For our purposes, this means knowing your prosperity path so clearly that it's effortless. That said, you may not be able to articulate it because it's like breathing for you. It's like saying to pull out a single piece of blue from the sky—it bends your mind to think about it.

Tuning in to your life purpose wisdom means increasing your awareness, your perception, around what's happening in your life. Notice where it feels good. Notice where something feels like a waste of your time. Unfortunately, we've been trained in the Western world to actually do the things we're not strongest in to build them up, which is counter-intuitive. For example, when in school, if math isn't a strong suit, you better study harder in math, get a tutor, and focus on getting good at it. But wait a minute—why? As an adult, you can outsource that skill. So focus on where you get the greatest joy. That is what allows you to express your purpose most clearly—where you can have the most fun and leave the biggest footprint.

Conversely, notice where you are moving away from your purpose. Your purpose is a guide in that everything is either bringing you closer or taking you away from it. Even in the midst of this grand pursuit, you still have to eat, get the laundry done, feed the family, and walk the dog. You are responsible for the details of living your life. So there's that . . . those other things will come up and get your attention. But if 90% of the time you're moving toward your purpose, you're going to be a lot happier. Which means the people around you are going to be happier. It means you're growing and in flow. You have synchronicity, feel supported, and trust what's happening in your life and business. You're in trust with yourself and with Source that you're going to be okay regardless of temporary circumstances (and it is all temporary), and that you're in authentic connection with other people.

Naiveté Can No Longer Be an Excuse

Sometimes learning and, therefore, knowing can feel like loss because now you're responsible for what you learn—you don't have the excuse of having naiveté there anymore. So sometimes discovering and knowing something can feel like a loss.

Also a lot of people will mistakenly put themselves in the category of knowing they don't know something because they haven't gotten any credentials for knowing what they know. People mistake credentials for knowing. It's important that teachers working with adults help them to claim credit for what they already know and what they can do without ever having realized it was valuable and worth something. Your clarity on that point goes a long way in establishing credibility with your clients.

It could be possible that we have a predetermined plan, life curriculum, or purpose, which our wisdom knows to use as navigation in life and business. We get to enjoy free will in making all the choices along the way and live the process. The good news is we can't ever get it wrong—it's only an experience. More importantly, it's our interpretation of our experience that determines quality of life and happiness.

We can use fear as a messenger of change. What is the fear of allowing X to happen? What's the fear of allowing a newspaper reporter in your dance class? What's the fear that prevents you from asking for your value in your pottery or coaching services or copywriting? What is the desire you want that triggers the fear to show up? When you're moving forward, it can trigger fear as you get near the edge of your status quo.

For example, if your desire is to be more visible, it can trigger fear—maybe nobody will want me to be a speaker, or if they did, I wouldn't know what to talk about, or I wouldn't be able to travel because of the pandemic. What is actually happening is that your fear is triggered as you get closer to your new unknown next best level. You can reverse engineer what's happening by thinking about the fear that comes up as you consider taking action. The bigger the fear, the more significant your perception about the action you are contemplating. What's the fear that comes up when you are moving toward or thinking about not changing toward what you want? What will the potential regret be if you don't take that action or change toward what it is you said you want?

To continue our example, what if our previously mentioned dance teacher didn't show up for her classes? The newspaper wouldn't cover her as the teacher. Those students would not get to be proud of their teacher. The newspaper's readers would not hear about her story. So think about the regrets and then ask, what's the payoff in having the fear stop me? Is that something you are willing to trade in to get what it is you said you want?

When you think of fear as a messenger of change and measure of significance, then it's not quite as scary anymore. Another good contemplation is to consider what is tied to your trust and belief in what is possible for yourself, your life, and your business. For example, if you want visibility but it can only happen in a certain way or through certain venues, you might have a self-imposed limitation. To what is your trust and belief tied to that affect your potential? Where are you limiting your possibility as a result of having a fear of the changes it would mean if you were actually successful in having what it is that you said you want? Think about what your beliefs are allowing or limiting as your possibilities.

Often people will say they know their wisdom work but it's so easy they're sure everybody can do it. First, just because it's easy to you does not mean it is not valuable. Secondly, when it's easy for you, it's your prosperity path. Ease means you're in the flow of you and what you can easily share with others.

Now there are people who know their wisdom but don't know that they know it and/or they can't express it. They describe it as "I can't put it into words," "I feel like I'm making it up," or "it's just a hunch." This can come from a fear of trying to put expertise into full expression because it could jeopardize what feels a little fragile as a knowledge base, or they might get ostracized or exiled for sharing something that's too far "out there." Or it might even be they would actually have to live up to what it is that they know so they limit their insights.

You may not be giving yourself credit for what you know or even be aware of what you know. Or you may have resistance around fully stepping into wisdom work for several reasons, all of which can be valid. However, wisdom work is all about transformation, for both your clients and yourself. You will be changed by the experience of enabling wisdom work to be your business.

Your Passions Are Fuel

Your passion is something you feel or have experienced. When you give your passion words, you allow your linear mind to get wrapped around it so you can take conscious action from it. It can inform your marketing, your language, and even your business systems.

Passion is a feeling state that is not an either/or—it's a both. Liking one particular thing is not necessarily passion; instead, it's an approach to life and business. Passion is usually inclusive and has other things associated with it. For example, if you are drawn to reading energy, you might also be drawn to creative problem-solving. Or if you find you are a natural healer, you might also be interested in physical wellness modalities.

Another aspect of passion is that you don't have to wait for the next big thing or for everything to be perfect and right before you can enjoy it. So often we are socialized out of our passion, being trained as children that it's more important to follow the rules than to live from our passion. As a result, passion can be a nebulous and unfamiliar experience. You might feel that creating prosperity from your wisdom is not worthy of passion or that it feels unrealistic. Unfortunately, that's a predictable response that is a by-product of living in our culture.

Knowing your passion is an important part of helping to understand your prosperity path. Passion can be tied to life purpose, which has two definitions as follows. We all share the first definition in that we're always getting closer to Source energy. We're here as a physical representation of the divine. The cosmos is living through us. So our job is to really go for it in every way we can and, essentially, report back our discoveries as we get closer to Source.

Now, there are times when we don't know how to articulate that so, instead, we focus on material things as a way to give us purpose. And when that doesn't serve, we look at the next material goal and so on. But those things can't satisfy us because it's not fulfilling our highest purpose of connection with source energy. So we can create some amazing results, but we don't really get to enjoy them because that's not what purpose is all about.

The second definition is that your purpose is your unique expression of your gifts, making tangible your potential in contribution to, and for, connection with others. It shows up regardless of circumstances, relationships, or situations, and it is always accessible to you. Essentially, it's your 'secret sauce.' This is a vital element of differentiating your prosperity path from anyone else's.

Your passion is what makes you, you. It's the fuel for your proverbial engine. It's not what other people think. It's not what they expect, what they project about you, or what they approve of . . . it's about your inner truth and how wisdom comes through you. Your passion isn't necessarily about what you do but why you do it. Your passions are the fuel that supercharges what you do in life and business.

Defining Wisdom

Now having context for why your 'wisdom work' is so important, and understanding that you must choose your opportunities as stepping stones to your next best level, it's time to explore a bit about your wisdom. (Then we'll put it all together to show you how to make a living from it.)

Contrary to what most people think, wisdom is NOT an accumulation of information, data, or facts. Instead, wisdom IS a state of being, a presence, and/or a way of interpreting the world around you. It's a feeling people get when they connect to you either physically or through your words, images, and videos via social media.

Take a moment to consider the people you would consider 'wise.' It's likely there's a sense of being grounded, of being compassionate, of security and appreciation for life, regardless of their profession or specialty. Often these are people who have suffered in some way. Age, gender, physical appearance…none of these things can tell you about the degree of wisdom that person holds; instead, it's how they communicate through their energy and their words.

Chances are others have reflected to you that you have wisdom. It may be honed in a specific life area, or for a particular audience, or to help others achieve a particular result. The key to your wisdom is how comfortable you are in embodying it, as that is what creates your state of being. (And your state of being is what creates your 'station,' or status, in life.)

In other words, when you embody, share, and teach wisdom, you are creating an energy that, eventually, manifests on the physical plane in some way. That will either be something for you (material possessions, a vacation, cash flow, etc.) or it will be something for someone else (your client's transformation, insight or paradigm shift that results in a different material world).

Either way, form *will* follow energy. Your wisdom is that energy.

Four Insights When You Act from Wisdom

There are four insights that will make a difference in your life when you follow your wisdom AND through which your wisdom will make a difference for your clients. Think of the following as the benefits your clients can experience through your wisdom work.

1. Possibility

First, there are possibilities. Who you consider yourself to be in your wisdom and its expression determines the range of possibilities you're open to and willing to consider for your life. If you don't know you can create a business by going and hanging out in Italy, then you have a natural limitation when thinking of going to Italy. But if you realize you could do such a thing, you increase the range of possibilities you're open to considering. And, from that mental space, you can make them happen. Henry Ford said, "Whether you think you can or you think you can't—you're right."

2. Clarity

The more clear you are, the more clear your life is in terms of making decisions and allocating your time and energy. You are responsible for what you're creating through your living and your business will reflect it. Having clarity supports your prosperity path.

3. Design

You can proactively design a life that is true and authentic as a reflection of your wisdom and life purpose. Transformation naturally occurs when you live into your wisdom fully. Again, you don't have to do anything special. There are no big rituals. Of course you can do rituals… but it's really about allowing the flow as you get into alignment with your wisdom.

4. Being

The focus is on your being, rather than the doing. There is no need to prove anything but, instead, about being in your life right now. The security is found in that which cannot be found outside of you. Said another way, you feel secure from the inside out and have no need to stay busy doing and looking to what's outside you for safety. When you are being, your life has richer context and meaning.

Your wisdom will support both you and your clients in powerful ways. So let's consider how to amp up your awareness.

GEENI Your Awareness

The five keys to awareness are perspective tools you can use to help sort out just about any situation, including enhanced awareness about your wisdom and prosperity path. I created this particular system when I went to work with Michael Gerber as a way to summarize what I'd seen for the probably seven or eight years at that point in my work with entrepreneurs. I named this system GEENI for Change as a play on words since you become your own genie in creating what you want in life and business. (Note: I eventually wrote a book on this subject called *You've Arrived!* in case you want to check it out further.)

The system has five keys, which can be used in any order. You don't need to start with the first one; instead, use your intuition to decide which key best suits the situation you're sorting out. For our purposes, you can apply them to discovering your prosperity path.

1. Greater Truth

The G in GEENI stands for Greater Truth. When you find yourself hitting speed bumps, resistance, things seem harder than they should be, or things aren't quite going right, or when you are getting blindsided with details, endings or opportunities, it means there is a Greater Truth at work. There is something bigger than you know that is trying to get your attention, and it's inviting you to step up. In that moment, you can take advantage of what that greater truth is trying to bring into your life.

For example, one of my clients quit her job after being employed there for twelve years. Previous to her job, she had tried running her own business but felt like she was running into brick walls. It didn't go well and a job seemed to be the right answer. But the longer she stayed at the job, the more she felt her spirit die and she quit. During our sessions, we explored where she wanted to go and what she wanted to do next. Her greatest passion was Italy, where she felt the freedom of unbridled romance with life; however, she had no idea she could create a business from that. That meant she completely discounted the brainstorming we did and she blew off any suggestions about anything Italy. It seemed too impossible.

When the possibilities became so overwhelming that she couldn't avoid them anymore, she took one small step, and then another, toward being in Italy. Today she is in Italy, putting together her new touring adventure package with the locals so Americans who want to experience Italian romance and food and art and good company get to go with someone who's all about it.

When there is a Greater Truth guiding your experience, it is a message that your wisdom is trying to bring you. In this case, it's around your ideal prosperity path.

2. Energy

The letter E in GEENI is for Energy. Energy is about what you feel in your body, your heart, your soul, and your life rhythms. When something doesn't feel right, it's a sign your wisdom is trying to express itself. Any 'off' feeling Energy is your messenger that something needs to be addressed in a different way to support you in claiming and acting from your personal best. If it doesn't feel right, it isn't . . . and this invitation for change can come up time and time again.

Several years ago, one of my clients was approached to do a joint venture with another business owner but just couldn't make the commitment to do it. It just never quite came together. She had no real reason other than it just didn't feel right. Months later, she happened to hear someone talking about the person who had initiated the joint venture and learned that person had done something unprecedented; essentially, that person had taken the money and run on several clients. That validated her read on the energy from her decision made months earlier. Fortunately, she had invested in cultivating business relationships she felt good about and had moved on in her business. The good news is she paid attention to the Energy and made a difficult decision that was at odds with what looked like a prime opportunity at the time.

So pay attention to the Energy that's happening in your world. See what's happening and how it feels to you before making any decisions. Consider potential outcomes based on how the Energy feels in the moment.

3. Environment

The second E in GEENI is for Environment. When the world around you is not reflecting who you are now, or you are having non-supportive or non-reciprocal relationships, or your physical world seems constrictive in any way, it's a clue that your best self is being contained or limited. You are playing small, or being kept small; sometimes this is about accommodating other people's comfort zones, but it's usually about your own. Just like the treatment for a sick fish is to treat the water, it's time to get your Environment handled so your wisdom can flow and your best self has room to show up.

One of my clients asked me if Environment extended to his truck. Naturally, I had to ask him the reason behind his question. In metaphysical terms, your vehicle is what takes you to where you're going so the Feng Shui of your car is that it is the vehicle, which moves your spirit in the physical world. My client happened to be a contractor who worked 12-hour days out of his truck. He was in his truck a lot more than average drivers. And he treated it that way. It was a hot mess—extra clothes, supplies, old food wrappers, water bottles, etc. After our session, he chose to clean it up. Predictably, he got three new jobs—large contracts—in the next ten days. It proved very advantageous for him to take care of the Environment of his vehicle.

Now was that coincidence or upgrading his Environment that got that result? In my world, there is a direct correlation between Environment and the experience a person has in life. Your Environment is more than physical space…it's the friends in your world, it's what you watch on TV, it's what you read, it's the ideas you think—it's anything that's in your personal fish tank around you. Your Environment has cues and clues about how your wisdom is expressing itself and how that flow or constriction is affecting your life.

Take a minute to look around you right now. What is the most prominent thing you notice? If it's a stack of hobby magazines in your office or notes on a new program you're creating or books you're meaning to get to, these are things that might say that your wisdom is sending you messages.

Where you put your attention is where you put your energy, even if it's in the "side" things because it's those that probably feel really good. And that's a clue to your prosperity path.

4. Natural Intelligence

The N in GEENI stands for Natural Intelligence. Your inner wisdom, which is a direct connection with universal consciousness, is always available and always supporting you in living your best life. The language of spirit is through pictures, intuition, and synchronicities. By paying attention to your Natural Intelligence, or wisdom, you're serving the universe as a physical expression of divine consciousness.

One of my clients was in her mid-forties and had to decide whether to sell her business or not, and it was a really emotional experience for her. She decided to just stop thinking about it and chose to not look at that decision because it was overwhelming. So what happened? First, she stopped making money in her business. Second, the Feng Shui of her home happened to have a bathroom in the area of her career area. The water pipes in her bathroom blew up and she had a big, huge flood (due to the suppressed emotional energy). Third, she started oversleeping for the first time in her life. She disengaged from everything to avoid the painful reality of making that decision. All these things were happening but she was ignoring them. That meant her Natural Intelligence had to be bolder. Within a couple of weeks after the burst pipes incident, a young woman walked in the front door of my client's business and asked if my client knew anyone selling a similar business because this woman's dream was to purchase a business instead of building it from scratch.

And *that* is synchronicity working with wisdom and one's prosperity path by helping get someone from where they are to where they need to be on their prosperity path. When you pay attention to, work with, and align your focus with Natural Intelligence, everything flows.

5. Integrity

Lastly, the I in GEENI stands for Integrity. By demonstrating consistency in what you say, do, and mean, you're in alignment with your truth. In this case, Integrity is not merely about being honest but is like the strength that is inherent in the hull of a boat that has Integrity. When a boat hull is out of Integrity, it leaks and, ultimately, sinks. When you are out of Integrity, your wisdom is limited because it has to work around the 'tweaked' area as an obstacle to your flow. Your best life can breathe when you are in Integrity in every way.

Continuing with the previous example, when my client started to oversleep, be irresponsible by ignoring her business decisions, and limit her possibilities to only what she thought was available to her in that moment, she had a lack of Integrity with her wisdom. That all affected her prosperity path because she stopped making money, which means she wasn't serving people by consistently delivering value anymore.

When you are in Integrity with your wisdom, there is cohesion in everything you do. Integrity makes your choices easier. It makes obstacles practically disappear because you don't get slowed down or stopped by them anymore. And you have clarity around how you are investing your time, energy, and resources.

To summarize the GEENI system, it is a way to access your wisdom from different perspectives. And it is a very personal journey. That's why you are here—to discover how to tune into and express your wisdom to benefit your prosperity path. Your wisdom gives your prosperity path meaning, direction, focus, clarity, a way to grow into all of who you are to be in this lifetime, *and* a way to make a good living.

As my gift to you, please visit this page to receive a complimentary multi-part email series on the GEENI for Change system: **http://geeniforchange.com/**.

Seven Signs of Not Listening to Wisdom

There are times when you might not listen to your wisdom for whatever reason; by understanding the signs that this is happening, you can course-correct as quickly as possible. And, bonus—these are some of the situations your wisdom work can help your clients overcome as well.

1. Repetitive Patterns

When you find yourself repeating patterns, it means you're not letting go of something—instead, you are reliving it over and over. Think Groundhog Day—you just re-treading the same situation with different names and faces. Over time (say, ten years), you are living your first year nine more times, or dating the same person with different names, or continuing to grapple with the same problem(s) you had last year, the year before, and the year before that. If something feels too familiar, it's an invitation to tune in and do something different to grow in new ways.

2. Living Behind Your Shields

When you are living behind your shields (or masks), you are numbing yourself to a situation, circumstance, or relationship. A shield could be perfectionism or addiction or obsession or substances or working all the time or watching too much TV... in short, a shield keeps you distracted from your priorities. They also keep you focused on 'out there' and other people instead of yourself.

There are masks that hold people back from knowing or living their wisdom. Some of those masks are being busy—the busy-ness factor—or other people's judgments, projections, or feeling 'not enough' so it's better not to even try. Another mask is about having to be perfect before being able to enjoy being purposeful according to their wisdom.

And then there is the mask of fear—flat-out, bald-faced fear. There's a Rumi quote about if the consequences fail to show up here, you can be sure they have taken form in the unseen. So many of us believe that . . . we prefer the choices we can see the results of but, often by the time they actually occur, it can be quite a long time later. That can apply to the case of feeling the power of your purpose because if you don't know quite what your purpose is, or you haven't really gotten to experience it and get stuck in love with the possibility of who you could become instead of trusting the power of your real self, you are really living in the not-expression of your purpose. You are living from that unseen place apart from the physical world.

When people think they can't move forward with their lives without knowing their life purpose, they become trapped. The truth is that purpose, and self-wisdom—are always there and showing up in some way. However, those trapped in this scenario have a mental illusion that doesn't allow them to experience the sweetness of their purpose in whatever form it's expressing right now because it's not showing up how they think it should be or what it should look like or that it's not like somebody else's so it's too far out of their frame of reference.

So when you have felt like you were tapping into your wisdom in the past, what did that feel like? Even if it was on purpose just for an event or for a day. People report that, generally, colors are brighter, life is lighter, the air is sweeter, and they are just happy. Sometimes you have to get rid of what wisdom isn't to know what wisdom is.. . meaning you need to let go of what it isn't in your mind so you can be open to what it is for you in this lifetime.

3. Re-Telling Your Story

When you are telling your story over and over and more and more, and then believing and living from it when it's a memory, you are not progressing as a result of your wisdom. For example, one of my clients started a new business, but was still regaling people with stories of being a Broadway dancer 20 years earlier. He entertained the dinner table with stories about directing a show or being exhausted from the dance vs. anything about his current business. He was re-telling his story long past its prime and, essentially, living in an echo.

Additionally, anytime you share your story and use the word "should," pay attention. We "should" on ourselves a lot—it's all of those things that we feel obligated to do, but never actually make the time for because, in truth, they aren't that important to us. When that word comes up, usually there's some sort of false obligation under that—some punishment or beat 'em up energy directed at self. "I should be doing something different. Why am I not doing that?" Should is a word that needs a 'to be used with caution' flag.

4. Interpersonal Conflicts

When you have interpersonal conflicts, meaning relationships that bump up against each other, or have unspoken negotiations, or feel consistently disappointed in someone else, it means something has not been clarified. It's another indicator that your purpose wisdom is being ignored. Your relationships should leave you feeling better more often than worse…there will be rough spots in any relationship (because that's how we grow stronger) but consistent conflicts mean you are missing something you need to make a better decision for yourself. Note that when you want a relationship to change, it does mean an ending; however, it could just be ending that chapter vs. the entire book.

For example, one of my clients was in a lengthy relationship of about six years. She and her (life and business) partner had weathered many life storms together—cross-country moves, career changes, financial scarcity, and more. However, they had come to a point when my client felt invisible and distant from her partner, which was not the relationship she wanted. She was quite upset when I suggested she plan for an ending. In fact, she was so upset that she didn't hear me when I said that she would benefit in the end by having the relationship she wanted—even if that was from her current partner in a new way. She did not handle this concept well (mostly because she couldn't hear me). It was, counter-intuitively, a measure of how much she loved her partner. She shared the insight she had received from this session with her partner, along with her anger and why she had wanted the session. As a result, she also shared clarity about what she wanted from the relationship. The partner had not understood any of it previously; this conversation completely shifted their relationship. They became closer and more abundant than ever before and are, to this day (as far as I know), still together.

We humans are social beings that grow through relationships with others. It's easy to simply cycle through to new relationships when we tire of the existing ones; however, the profound connection that is afforded by working through those moments by speaking truth with compassion for self and others is truly wondrous. Trusting your wisdom to help you along the way will change everything.

5. Illness or Injury

When you experience physical illness or injury, your body is taking the hit for something you should know and act on accordingly. When you are not in full wellness, your body is actually trying to stop you so you can get out of confusion or resistance and back on track.

One of my clients realized something big was off with her when she didn't listen to her physical body. She had a rash on her left hand for several weeks, and it kept spreading from stress. She had to look back at what the triggering event might be and discovered she felt she couldn't get what she deserved financially from her clients. Metaphysically, the left hand is about receiving while the right hand is about giving; knowing that, you can look to see if you have imbalances in giving and receiving.

The body never lies. It knows things that have yet to be articulated mentally. Anything that happens to us has to go through several levels—through the spiritual level, the emotional level, the intellectual level, and finally ends up at our physical body. By the time it manifests on the physical level as a symptom, it's been in our energy field for a while. When you have a physical symptom, you want to look at the metaphysical cause of what's happening.

Most often, I've noticed that 'red' conditions are related to anger, being upset, and/or being really unhappy. If something is happening in your physical body, especially when repetitive, it's an invitation to look deeper at what's happening around you and in your life.

One of my clients kept getting sick with a bad cold, over and over. She would get better for a couple days, then be right back in bed sick. She was upset because she was doing a lot of healing and clarity work and thought she should be feeling lighter and better. Instead, she was detoxing energy. She needed to slow down because she was being effective in her release work; her body was deluged with toxic release and needed time to catch up with her newfound clarity.

If you find you have knee issues, that's about changing direction, family relationships, and/or related to your ego around stepping out in the world. Hip issues are about money. When you walk, you are moving your hips, which means you are moving money energy. So when you need more money, take a walk.

Stress can be cumulative, meaning your body can take it for a while and, after a certain amount of time, your body just needs a break—which it will take one way or another. Taking action toward what feels good and stepping into your purpose and claiming the power of it is a way to handle stress. When you start getting multiple issues, either that's one message being delivered repetitively or it's several messages that have created a backlog in your physical body.

6. Self-Sabotage

Another sign of avoiding, marginalizing, ignoring, or even negating your purpose wisdom is self-sabotage, or what I call manufactured speed bumps. That phrase stuck with me from a trip to Jamaica years ago, when I learned natives called speed bumps "sleeping policemen." So if you manufacture your speed bumps to 'govern' your speed, meaning you find yourself banging into walls and sabotaging what's happening, you're missing or mis-using your life purpose wisdom.

When you are unable to be consistent with expressing your life purpose, there's something underneath that. So where is the priority that supersedes living your life purpose? Sometimes there's a sense of obligation, which may not be as real as you think it is, or it may be a very real sense of responsibility in terms of taking care of family.

The consistency in living your life's purpose is relative. Where it becomes an issue is when it feels like you're not enough in some way.

Or, conversely, if you've taken great steps and you're really close to reaching for a big pay-off, you might find you become inconsistent as a way to sabotage and not allow yourself the risk of going for that reward. Sometimes we think we should be in a different place than where we are by this point in our lives but the truth is that, if that were true, we would be in that place. And yet, it's also a sign of a person being off-track with where they are meant to be and what they're doing and who they are in life.

Fear can be a powerful saboteur. The good news is you can use fear as the milestone of your personal growth because fear only shows up where you are taking action. And it makes total sense. When you are going beyond where you've been, you don't know what is out there. It's only natural to be on high alert and poised to handle the worst.

Altogether, any of the shields—busy-ness, watching a lot of tv, being distracted by others, etc.—are self-sabotaging behaviors that keep us from living our true purpose.

7. Trying to Be Who You Used to Be

Here is a relatable story about how living from who you used to be happens every day. A woman had gained weight over many years but still had clothes from being a smaller size way back when. This woman pulls out these small sized clothes to remind herself she can be that small again. She's in love with the person that she isn't—and she loathes the person she is—because she's overweight. She punishes herself with negative self-talk and a promise that, when she loses the weight, everything will be perfect. Her choice is about existing in the unseen world, and yet, her physical world experience depends completely on whether she can lose enough weight to make it be what she dreams it to be while she hates her body. Her physical world becomes a prison of despair with her weight being the warden of her prison. She can't hate her way to health and, yet, she can't live in her present either. Instead, she needs to live from who she is today.

Those are the seven signs of ignoring your life purpose wisdom—repeating patterns, living behind the shields, telling your story over and over and living from it, interpersonal conflicts, physical illness or injury, self-sabotage, and trying to be who you used to be (vs. who you are today).

As you well know (you wisdom worker, you), intuition is not judgmental, it is always present, and it is dynamic, meaning it is ever-accessible and evolves with the rhythms of life. The only intent of intuition is to give you guidance to reach your next best level in life and business. It can be destabilizing to reach for something larger than you thought you were ready for… but, every time, intuition is about bringing into reality that which you seek. Trust what your intuition shows you to enable expression of your deeper wisdom in and through your work.

Remember, you can also reference these seven signs as indicators or situations that clients could address and resolve as benefits of working with you.

Working from Your Wisdom

Once you are accessing your wisdom, there is typically an uptick in the way you see things. For example, your capacity for putting up with failure, rejection, or tedium increases dramatically, because you now have a very strong and compelling reason to overcome potential obstacles. Your wisdom becomes your prosperity path. With an authentic, compelling, and purposeful prosperity path, fewer (and smaller) obstacles will have the ability to slow or stop you in creating the results you desire.

For myself, I am compelled to translate energy (energy being the messenger of the Universe) into something people can use on a practical level. I choose to do it with (would-be) entrepreneurs because I have an affinity there. Anybody who chooses to be a wisdom worker and create their prosperity path accordingly is hearing a calling. They are not interested in living between the lines of a job. There is a special kind of heart, a courage, and a commitment that transcends what most people would be willing to do with and in their lives. When I started this work in 1998, I was wayyyy ahead of the curve. I risked social rejection, financial security, and my own well-being to create my prosperity path from my wisdom. When I look back now, every risk I took was worth it. (I would do some things differently because I've learned along the way . . . my intention now is to save other wisdom workers from taking the 'scenic route' in living from their prosperity path.)

At any rate, when you are living from your wisdom and actively engaged with helping others through your distinctive prosperity path, you'll know it. It feels good. Time flies. Your work flows. You have resilience when meeting and resolving challenges. You magnetically attract opportunities and relationships and business. You contribute more fully to the world around you. And it's something you would do whether or not money is attached to it. The key is to create a business model that ensures you get paid when you share your wisdom with your clients and students.

Your wisdom provides an ongoing context, a guiding energy, that doesn't stop when you achieve success with your prosperity path. And it helps you discover, sort out, and achieve bigger things. For example, one of my clients was trying to figure out what she wanted to do with her life. Her father convinced her to become an engineer for career stability because that was important to him. She thought it made sense so she decided to get a good education as an engineer. After graduating, she got good jobs as an engineer for a lot of years— decades, in fact. And she was miserable the whole time. As a result, she quietly gained weight, and gave away her power by not saying no to people and projects that didn't feel right. She did whatever anybody said when they needed it. She was ignoring her wisdom and created a prosperity path that had a high price tag—her own quality of life and life satisfaction.

Eventually, being so unhappy led to being in debt as well as miserable, she quit her job. She took time to remember her childhood dream to work with the sea and its animals. She recalled that the ocean comforted her and that she used to sketch wildlife. She realized her ideal prosperity path is tied to protecting the oceans and supporting animals to thrive in their natural habitats. Applying her engineering background, she chose to promote oceanic health. She moved across the country to a state that offers relevant education on that subject and which has a shoreline. She gained new opportunities to consult, as well as resources and connections to help her live her dream. And it all happened very quickly . . . within a few months after decades of languishing on the wrong prosperity path. Once she honored her wisdom, she made powerhouse decisions and took action on her knowingness. That same potential exists for you as well.

Purpose Leads
to Prosperity

In the book, *Atlas Shrugged* by Ayn Rand, one of the main characters is asked, "What is the most depraved kind of human being?" His answer would likely surprise most people because it wasn't a murderer or a rapist—it was the man without a purpose. When the author was asked why she suggested this as opposed to other possibilities, she replied because that characteristic lies at the root of the cause of all the evils—sadism, dictatorship, or any form of evil. She believed lack of purpose is the result of man's evasion of reality and failure to think. A man without purpose is at the mercy of spontaneous feelings or unidentified impulses and is capable of any evil because he is, as a result, totally out of control of his own life. So to have control of your life and prosperity path, it is important to have a productive purpose.

Additionally, one of the things we mortals must remember, as our lives are filled with being busy doing things, is that just because you *can* do something doesn't mean you *should*. In fact, it's an inversely proportional relationship: as busy as you are is as overwhelmed as you feel. Which means it feels like the busier you are, the more you feel you need to be doing to get everything done. It's a vicious cycle. As hard as you push to get everything on your to do list done is as many more things you discover that need to get done. (Actually, that's probably the universal law of attraction, the law of attention and the law of reciprocity all at work there, but that's for another time....)

The goal is to be both purposeful and on purpose instead of just busy. It is vital to know what you love, what you are good at, and what people will pay you for solving. You are not as good at some things as you are at others, and there are people who are really good at the things you are not. By continuing to do the things you are not as good at, you are burning out your energy and are actually withholding opportunities for people who are really good at those things to do them.

So, by *not* allowing people to do those things they do really well (which are the same things that you do not do well), you are actually blocking your own energy and taking time away from the things that you, and only you, do really well. And if you don't do the things that only you can do, they will never see the light of day and actually get done. And that would be the biggest travesty of it all.

Your purposeful expression waits for you, and it is always expressing itself in some form or another. For me, my life purpose is about getting closer to what I call 'Source' energy—that which is essential and authentic about a person. Often we don't know how to articulate that, so instead we focus on material things but, when that doesn't serve, we look at the next material goal and so on...but those things can't satisfy us because it's not fulfilling our highest purpose of connection with source energy.

When you are purposefully expressing your truth in a viable business model, there is an energy, a resilience, a flow to and through your work. You naturally attract the right relationships, resources, and opportunities. You are able to contribute more fully to your clients and your own business results. That all requires being more intentional, more purposeful, and more aligned with your wisdom to benefit your prosperity path.

In being more intentional with your time, energy, and resources, there are triggers for understanding what you do not need to do anymore to be in integrity with your purposeful expression (aka in this case, prosperity path): knowing when you are too busy with your to-do list and yet adding to it, when you are feeling the emotional pinch between being a mere human and your ever-growing to-do list, when you get things done that weren't even ON your to-do list in the first place . . . these are the messages to know it's time to figure out what things you don't need to do anymore so you can stay on track with your true purpose (the things that only you can do—like deliver your wisdom as a service, create new ideas, and help your clients remember who they are to get more of what they want on a deeper level).

I believe every single person has the capacity to pull in what they need to grow. Sometimes recognizing that happens in opposition . . . meaning, you might not know your purpose but you know what it isn't.

Your unique purpose—that which you are called to do in a way that only you can do—is not found outside of you but is something within you. It's not a big production. It's something that feels really easy and natural—so much so that it can be overlooked. It's not urgent but it's deeply important. It's not some sort of bliss where you float around in Lotus position ohm-ing all the time and nothing bad ever happens to you. It's not a job (although it could be about how you do your job!). It's also not material accumulation. It's not how much stuff you have no matter how awesome your stuff is and how much you love it.

Your purpose is also not invented. Your purpose is very sincere and authentic. Your purpose is always waiting for you. It's always expressing itself in some form or another. So your unique expression of your gifts, making tangible your potential in the physical world, which ideally is in contribution to and for connection with others, will show up regardless of circumstances, relationships, or situations. Your purpose is always accessible to you.

Your purpose is not something you do—it's the reason you do things. Your life purpose is always right there, guiding you, informing you of your right next actions. But when you can't see your purpose, it could be because of conditioning or judgment or limited thinking. I worked with a client who has this amazing unique talent as a potter—she makes one of a kind ceramic pottery. It takes her about 15 hours to create each piece. And she's selling these pieces for just $35. These are works of fine art! She is an example of someone who doesn't know the value of the result of their passion, reinforced by people in her world who advised her to drop her prices so she could sell more.

Your purpose is not found outside of you—it's not about your goals or relationships with other people or a false sense of security. When you have assumptions or expectations or other people's projections around who you should be or what you should be doing, it will take you off-purpose. How you know you're in alignment with your life purpose is when you're feeling the flow, and opportunities are coming to you, and you have a lot of vitality and high energy. You're able to make positive choices for yourself in the moment. You can use your resources toward what you want consistently because you know what your purpose is, and that it will guide you to your prosperity, so you can spend money to feed your spirit. You know why you're going to spend money. Money is just an energy that fuels your desire and happiness and fulfillment of your purpose.

Without purpose, you're going to be pulled in different directions. You're not going to be able to engage in your business because it's good enough the way it is so you might think 'why do something different or work harder?' You won't have the handle on what makes you happy or prosperous. It might cause a feeling of 'if only'—'if only it was perfect like X', you'd be off doing it. The truth is that you are where you need to be right now, in this moment. If your purpose needed you to be somewhere else, you would be there. So it's always only perfect. It's always about choosing your direction—whether you're moving toward or away from your purpose, toward or away from your natural prosperity, toward or away from your happiness and contentment.

Most people want something more from their prosperity path. When you know your purpose, you're able to enjoy greater abundance from the flow that will benefit your business.

There are people along the way who are your teachers. Sometimes your greatest teachers are the ones you have the most struggle with because they're the ones who are showing you where your magic is by opposition. The greater the pushback, the greater the power.

It can feel selfish to live your life purpose, especially in the face of caring for others or doing what others expect, want, or need. We are socialized to take care of everyone and everything else except ourselves (or, at least, to put ourselves last). To live your purpose, especially for your prosperity path, can feel selfish. In that moment, it's important to remember that investing in your life purpose and living from it is probably the biggest contribution you can make to yourself and others. While it's the most significant role model you can be for the people in your world, at the same time you risk breaking the social context of the communities in which you are a member. When living on purpose while your friends think you should be doing something different or are judging your purpose or prosperity path in some way, you may have to leave some of those relationships or communities. They may not be able to go with you as you move to your next purpose-driven level. You definitely are risking social context when you live beyond and into your purpose. It's important to be mindful of that possibility.

The Four Energy Drains You Can Avoid

Should there be a time when your life feels stuck, boring, or you're trying too hard for too little progress, you are not harnessing the power of purpose to help make it happen. So you've probably been focused on creating from a needs base or survival place and where we put our attention is what we create. When your attention is focused on not having enough money, that's what you get more of—not enough money. However, when you're in alignment with your purpose, everything flows and it's easy. The outcomes are byproducts of the fulfillment you feel everyday by living purposefully.

When you're not living and working on purpose, you experience what I call the Four Energy Drains—discontent, disconnect, disharmony, and dis-ease. Dis-ease can be physical (because your body takes the hit for it) or it can be dis-ease with your life in terms of resistance, old beliefs, or negative patterns. Maybe you need to know more and more and more before you can do anything or you tend to stay in overwhelm or drama to avoid making a real shift. Or maybe you don't know your value. Or maybe you're not ready to do something significant because you're not sure how it would actually change your life or it would require new and unfamiliar habits to attain it. So you prepare to prepare so you can be prepared. Or you're attached to the outcome instead of actually being present in the process of achieving and having what you want using your purpose as a compass. These are all guideposts you can use when you know what to look for along the way in creating your optimal prosperity path.

At the same time, the Four Energy Drains are the same access points you can use to influence your energy, create something new, and get more of what you want in your life and business. Struggle is the process of getting into alignment with your wisdom; by paying attention to what feels good and what doesn't, you're using the most basic part of your anatomy—your awareness—as the natural compass you were born with to create more alignment and integrity in your life. This leads living into your optimal prosperity path.

My clients describe being out of alignment with purpose in life or business being a burden—heavy, dark, intense, like hard work to get even small wins, like you're waiting for something to happen to get what you want. Wins feel far away. You might feel trapped in your life and business. There might be a sense of overwhelm because you have information you're not able to apply or you just don't or something gets in your way of being able to take a particular action. There's a lack of clarity. Fears are running your life or your business. And you're likely not taking care of yourself either. That can be punishment because you don't deserve the best, or maybe you haven't earned putting yourself as a priority yet, or you might be feeling a lack of control in your life. There are many reasons that vary by the individual; no matter what, too many people get stuck in such scenarios because they believe them to be real and permanent. However, when you trust yourself and Source, anything is possible.

It's a disservice to you (and others) if you are in a business that isn't connected with your purpose, passion, or natural talents. Things get distorted when alignment is missing. Maybe you have only a vague sense that you should be doing or being something different. Maybe you don't know what to do next but want to honor what you have already created. Maybe you need to find ways to verbalize your wisdom into language that makes sense to potential clients.

Not knowing your purpose is like having the gift of eyesight while being locked in a black room with a trick door. That door can be right in front of you but you can't see it and you don't know how to unlock it. You don't know how to get out of the dark. Knowing your purpose and how to state it clearly can find, unlock, and open the door for you and your prosperity path.

In working with clients over the years, I have learned that too often people are not sure of what they know—instead they focus on what they don't know. That is a sure way to stay stuck and distracted because their business does not progress in that scenario. Sometimes they rely on other people understanding them, even if they can't articulate the value of their wisdom themselves. It shows the importance of relationships with others to see yourself as well as the need to cultivate self-wisdom.

The lure of your prosperity path can be a paradox. You find it by being more authentically yourself and following your own wisdom. By being committed to your personal transformation in understanding yourself, your wisdom and your business model better, you'll be more productive, more efficient, and better able to take advantage of opportunities to come along. You are poised to create your own economy.

Working from your purpose for your optimal prosperity path gives you clarity in what you do, with consistency. Things feel easy, like breathing. Your purposeful expression also creates an environment that feels supportive. It facilitates resource attraction. And, most importantly, it is your wisdom expressing itself from the inside out.

How Your Purpose Shows Up for Prosperity

Your life purpose shows up in everything you do because it's your values, your beliefs, your emotions, your actions, and your results. There's a whole life cycle there. Your values tell, show, demonstrate, or lead you to believe what you believe. Your beliefs will help determine how you feel about whatever that is. Your emotions are what prompt you to take action. And then the actions are what create the results in the physical world. It all starts with your purpose and values going into beliefs. In other words, it's the intangible that creates the tangible. When you're aligned with your purpose, your results have greater clarity in your relationships, career, money, communication, creativity, community reputation... in short, your prosperity path.

It's easy to get excited when feeling purposeful; however, purpose is different than the adrenaline doing it generates. It's not just that 'high,' although the rush is a part of it. Instead, your purpose generates an energy that is much deeper than that surface adrenaline. Just as being efficient isn't always effective, and being effective isn't always from effort, and profits don't come from potential alone, results come from being in alignment with your purpose and taking action. It's about harnessing the power of you into physical expression.

Another way to think about your purpose is to look at your childhood fantasies way back when for clues about your purpose. One of my clients recalled a childhood scenario she replayed over and over again where she was a preacher... as an adult, when she added public speaking to her business, she naturally attracted more clients. Another client had a Barbie doll that had lots of new adventures without worrying about the clothes or the car or how she looked... today she is an entrepreneur, having lots of adventures, living in her jeans. So think back to how your life purpose showed up in the only language you had when you were a kid as another tool for insight.

Another point about how your life purpose shows up is that it is not about skill, which is learned, but about your talent or natural ability. You likely learn the skills related to your natural ability easily; from there, you can polish them. The bigger idea is you expand your natural talents as the flow state of your life. The greatest act of love available for you is when you are living into your purpose because that gives other people the permission to live their purpose as well. You being authentically you is what allows other people to be authentic as well.

Your purpose affects every decision you make in your life. It is who you are being versus what you are doing. It will let people know your true North, where you're going, and helps you know your right direction at the same time. Your purpose lets people experience your worldview. Your purpose is a factor in what makes you unique. We love the differences in each other and others love what makes us unique as part of our purpose.

When you don't know the purpose of, well, anything, you don't do it as well as you could because you don't understand the bigger why. But when you know the why behind you doing what you're doing, you're on purpose. The same is true with your life path.

When you are in alignment with yourself, you can get traction and build momentum; however, when you don't know why you're doing something, whatever you're doing will feel disjointed and fractional. You've got to know why you're doing what you're doing to support and possibly even clarify your purpose.

Consider your current commitments—the ones you actually follow through on—to see how your purpose is showing up. Where you invest your time, energy, and resources is a reflection of your purpose. Your commitments tell you what's important to you. Are you at the gym daily? Do you write your new book project every weekend? Do you take time to talk to your neighbors regularly? Look at how your purpose is showing up in terms of where your attention goes as a real-world focus for what's important to you.

Being on purpose will actually give you energy because you get more done faster when fueled by natural passion. It's what compels great achievements. Nothing great has ever been achieved because it was an obligation or on a 9–5 time clock. Great achievements are almost always a labor of love that are inspired and compelled in some way. It comes from spirit as a direct conduit of some aspect of purpose—individual or collective.

So when the going gets tough, do you focus or do you fold? When you're in your purpose, you're focused and going for it so it's unlikely you are going to crumple or give in when things get a little rigorous. So often we're socialized to operate from what 'was' (our history), or what society's judgment considers normal, which means handling challenges in traditional ways. For me, I've been focused on being a catalyst long before I became one professionally. I just did what felt right as I went. Other people looked at me like I had a third head. My friends wondered why I didn't just go get a job, or settle down with a husband who could support me. But that wasn't my path—at least, up until now. I love what I do and I know I'm on purpose.

Your feelings are your emotional body sensations of what's happening, which can be clues to shifts in your purpose and your consciousness. Pay attention to how you're feeling in a given moment to know when you're on purpose. When it feels right, you're happy, time is flying . . . those are signs you're in your flow.

A Key Question

A question that might help pull out your purpose is: if you had everything taken care of, how would your life be different? If everything was handled, where would you be focusing your time? Would you be making beadwork, feeding the hungry or traipsing jungles to discover new medicines? Where would you focus your time and attention?

Your purpose is the thing that only you can do the way you do it. If there's other stuff in the way of expressing your purpose, whether it's cleaning your house or running your errands, then offload it. If you find yourself spinning your wheels and not knowing what to do next, that can be one of the masks we wear when we're too busy or need clarity. Sometimes that is a distraction to test us or it can be that we are overly involved where we shouldn't be at all. It's a disservice to everyone when you're not in alignment with your purpose.

Sometimes your purpose gets buried under all kinds of stuff that isn't even yours—inherited limitations, mental conditioning, habitual actions, projections from others or duplicated patterns you picked up from your parents or authority figures. So just keep asking yourself: is what I'm doing right now the right thing to help me become or express all of who I am?

Other questions you can ask yourself include the following. Am I distracting myself? Am I avoiding feeling or thinking or handling something? Am I complaining about something? Am I blaming someone or something? Am I somehow numbing out? Am I self-medicating? Am I annoyed or cranky or irritated? Am I upset I haven't enforced or honored one of my own boundaries? That's a good one because boundaries don't come from outside. If somebody does something that steps on you, they don't know it—that's your responsibility.

You teach people how to treat you. That becomes much more clear when we know our purpose. When you know you are valuable and you have a purpose, it makes it easier to enforce that boundary with other people. Ask yourself if you are avoiding someone? Are you avoiding doing something or avoiding a situation? Where are you avoiding, procrastinating, or feeling under-prepared?

These kinds of questions allow you to dig under the face of the situation so you can get to what I call 'the work.' You have to understand what's really happening to get at the source causing the current circumstance. When you can address it at its source, which is the only place you can actually create sustainable change, you give yourself the gift of choice. You want and need to get underneath whatever is happening on the surface to what's really going on to create upshift and transformation. Through it all, keep asking, "Am I doing the right thing now to help me become or express all of who I am?" "Is this the best use of my time, energy, and resources to get me to where I want to go?"

I worked with a client who wanted to do everything all by herself. She committed to following the answers she got when she asked herself these questions. When the answer was no, she wasn't doing the right thing, she did something different—even if she wasn't comfortable with it. As a result, she met new people, attracted new clients, and revitalized her perspective. It was a bit like that movie with Jim Carrey where he had to say yes to everything…she chose to do something different whenever she got a no. And her life and business transformed as a result.

I have another client who happened to discover she's a perfectionist as a result of this exercise. And it drives her boyfriend nuts because she always felt the need to explain herself, to defend her reasoning for doing things. She needed to explain why things didn't go the way she wanted and she didn't realize she did that over-explaining with everything. She realized she needed to make sure the other person was okay with what really happened. She saw she was trying to 'own' their experience and manage their emotional response. This is more common than you might think, especially with purpose-led people who are soul-driven, compassionate, and intelligent. It's not what we choose to do—we just do it. We take care of others. We nurture them. It's who we are vs. what we do.

Many service-based professionals unconsciously operate at this level and don't know they are abdicating their own boundaries and preferences to prevent others from being upset. For example, they may hold back on speaking their truth if they think it will hurt someone. That self-editing is not trusting the other person to have their own response and take care of themselves. That's not trusting Source to be there for them. And it's actually sabotaging their potential growth opportunities. It removes their ability to use their own discernment, feel their feelings, and make a decision. When you handle an issue for another person for them before it even gets to them, that person can't grow from the experience; instead, they will have to repeat that experience. The bad news is it will likely be bigger, badder, and bolder because they didn't get it the first time.

Life Purpose Formula

This Life Purpose Formula is something I put together to give words to the amorphous experience in your energy field when you're thinking about your life purpose. It's a formula of exactly one sentence with three fill-in-the-blank sections.

"My true life purpose is to share _____ (*natural talent, wisdom, or gift*), so that _____ (*who or what*) will experience _____ (*the result you expect will occur*)."

The reason it focuses on others benefitting from your life purpose is because, in the end, we are all walking each other home. Our purpose expresses through our relationships with others.

As an example, here is the Life Purpose Formula statement from one of my clients. "My life purpose is to share my ability to see beneath the surface of people's problems and challenges so that people who are frustrated and in life pain can achieve their goals and have the happiness and wealth they truly want." When you're stating your purpose and your dream so clearly, there's no room for doubt or fear because it will pull you forward into action. Here is another example: "My life purpose is to share the distilled life experience, wisdom and expertise in translating the messages from the Universe so entrepreneurs who want to operate their businesses from their soul's wisdom will make a bigger contribution and a good living at the same time."

Try it out and see what comes through as truth for you.

The Prime Directive

Another tool you might want to use is what I call the Prime Directive. Here's the formula:

"I know I'm successful by _____."

For example, mine is: I know I'm successful by the degree of positive transformation I facilitate in, for, through, and with the people around me. I've lived by that for decades. It's why I get up in the morning—to facilitate positive transformation. I really want to help people actualize their potential and get to be all of who they are in their magnificence. I happen to do it quite often with entrepreneurs because they have a special quality, a commitment to going above and beyond because they know what's riding on it. That pulls them forward even if they don't know they're ready for it. That said, I am ecstatic when I can help anyone facilitate transformation—when they're ready to shift and want help to make it easier, I'm all about it.

One of my clients used this Prime Directive to state she knew she was successful because she helped her clients create change—and she was criticized for it. Whoever criticized her said something like she was looking for her validation through another person. Fortunately, she did not get sucked into that trap because when people judge someone that quickly, they've either got something up that was triggered by that person or it's a mirror teaching us something profound.

In this case, it could be that my client was used to getting the beat-down (from others or herself) so she naturally called someone in to do it for her. When a harsh reflection comes back that fast, especially when you feel it as a sting, ping, or a charge, that is a sign there's a hidden truth in it somewhere, whether or not you know what it is and whether or not you approve of it. It's an invitation for you to look further, to see the magic under that message. Ask if there is a truth in it for you; if there wasn't, it would not have found a landing place within you. It couldn't stick unless it found a soft spot within you.

In that moment, you could also (depending on how well you know that person) state a summary of the situation to pull clarity out of what's happening. "It seems my words really provoked a response so let's have dialogue about that."

Usually the Prime Directive is my private mantra and my Life Purpose Formula is my true and public purpose. But you need to play with those tools to see what is right for you. Once you put your formulas together, break the words into their elements. For example, if you use the word 'spiritual', what does that really mean for you? Does spiritual mean you shaved your head and wear orange robes or that you go to church every day or that you don't because the world around you is your church?

Explore how you want your purpose to reveal itself as well. Do you want to float around and bump into it? Do you want it to flow through you whether or not you know it? Do you want the straight path, the curving path, or any path? You get to choose your experience. Do you want to grow through strength and resilience or just take the express route? Make your life purpose feel vital, distinctive, and personal. If someone else can say the same statement about their life purpose and it makes sense for them, then it's not really juicy enough for you. Define your 'who' with care…choose your adjectives for what they mean on deeper levels…do not take this for granted.

It's significant work to be able to state your life purpose in a way that has clarity, resonance, and meaning.

Through this kind of deep work, one of my clients discovered she was an organizer. She thought everybody just organized stuff. She judged her ability to organize as not important enough and not really valuable. After she did her homework to articulate, claim, and really 'own' her purpose as an organizer in service to others, she had clients lined up for weeks!

The Four Most Important Things You Can Do

Here's something you need to know...you won't grow by being comfortable. When you're comfortable, you cruise along with what's working. It's only when you are uncomfortable in some way, where you want something different, that you will look around to see what's going on.

So where you are unhappy is actually the gateway to greater fulfillment. And I'll say that again, where you are unhappy is actually the gateway to greater fulfillment. Your soul is trying to show you what isn't working and it may be doing a lot to get your attention. What it really means is the place where you aren't in alignment with your purpose is where your purpose is looking for a way to express itself. In the moment of unhappiness, it is not happening in some way. Something needs to change—either new decisions going forward or, at least, finding a way to avoid ending up in the same places in the future.

For example, I have a client who was very successful in his career, in the automotive industry. He's been in the car business for his entire professional life. He's risen to the top of the ranks to have his own dealership. And then he got to be an even bigger General Manager (GM) guy. And he would spend some of his time just hanging out on the floor, the sales floor, talking with customers and selling a car every now and again,; he just loved selling cars. And when he talked about selling cars and creating new dealerships, his eyes would light up and then he would get back to his regular day and the light would go out just a little.

Eventually, he lost the job due to changes in the economy. It was painful. It's also a sign that he's a connector. He's a person-to-person, heart-to-heart connector, and he enjoys the creating part of something new. He's not meant to work for someone else to farm someone else's field. He's meant to make tangible something that has yet to be born and to connect with people in a personal way where he gets to help them get what they want. So being a big GM guy took him too far away from his people and from the magic of creation. As a result, his soul changed his world so he could revisit his life purpose.

We each create our own path to get where we need to go. So look at your current life challenges and ask, how is your life purpose speaking through them? When you start to recognize that the magic is in the message, you give yourself the opportunity to grow faster. By getting out of resistance and into curiosity about what's happening and why you're creating it empowers you to notice and express something significant for your purpose. So take a minute to slow down and look at it from a different new perspective. If what you see is frustration (or negativity or anxiety or stress or, or, or), ask yourself what it would take for that state to be its opposite—to be fulfilled or to feel good? Why? Because that is the direction your life purpose is trying to pull you toward.

Here are four simple things you can do to help discover and life into your life purpose.

1. Listen to your own inner guidance for next action steps; know what you know and then follow through on that knowledge.

2. Connect with like-spirited people who understand and can offer meaningful support.

3. Everything counts. Make sure you are being and doing things in the most effective use of your time, energy, and resources in every moment to move toward your purposeful prosperity.

4. Have a current, strategic, functional, relevant, realistic business vision map in place. This is a tool I use with my clients to synthesize where they are, where they want to be, and how they are going to get there. Whatever you use to plan your business growth, be sure it accurately reflects your purpose.

If you get nothing else out of this, you already know more than you did before you started reading. Your life purpose is 'right there.' At the same time, we often can't see it due to conditioning and judgment and limited thinking and assumptions and expectations and projection about what it should be according to what other people think.

Another quick example of that: I was working with a client who jokingly said her purpose seemed to be organizing things—closets, gardens, billing systems, etc.—but she had decided that was not an important enough gift to celebrate or follow through on for a business. I asked what she wanted her life purpose to be; her answer was, well, "I wanted to be Mother Teresa." (And, of course, that 'job' is already taken...)

Your purpose is significant because it's uniquely yours. You have something within you that is easy and simple to express in the world. That is your natural prosperity path.

The Unexpected Gateways of Change

Pay attention to your passions, your fears, your saboteurs, the resistance in all its forms ... look for those as the unexpected gateways to change. Consider who you hang out with ... what you watch / read

...where you invest your time, energy, and resources. Where do you feel good after you've had an experience (a relationship, an outing, a phone call, a business gig, etc.)—and where do you feel 'less than' (like you gave too much)? What are your life threads—those things that seem to be present throughout your life? What do people share with you about their experience of you? Ask yourself the big question as previously shared—am I doing right now the right thing to help me become or express all of who I am? Play with your Life Purpose Formula and your Prime Directive statement.

So look in your proverbial mirror to see how your purpose might be showing up. Look to see how your inner world is reflecting in your outer world or in what ways your outer world is simply a reflection of your inner world. Look around you for the commonalities that will tell you more about what's happening in your world. Consider your relationships, especially new ones, to see what you're putting out. Consider your habits, your purchases, your food habits, your conversations, your ideas, your career...for example, if you find you have the same kinds of friends or your friends have the same kinds of interests or habits, that's a thread. If you find you are attracting clients with money issues, how is your money? Are you in scarcity in some way? What you attract is a key to the energy you are running and the frequency of your purpose as it's moving through, or you are allowing it to move through, your life and business.

For example, I really don't have many people in my world who have a job. I'm all about entrepreneuring. So I see entrepreneurs, visionaries, creators, leaders, innovators, people who are willing to risk who they are and what they know to help others and live with a degree of freedom that can be terrifying for others. What's out there is a physical reflection of what's happening inside my energy field.

As a side note, it took a long time for me to get these things figured out and distilled into what feels really simple. The greatest sophistication is simplicity. Blaise Pascal, a famous writer, once said he would have written a short note but, because he didn't have time, he had to write a long letter. Editing something into simplicity takes time. Original thinking also takes time and it is not easy—plus it challenges what you think you already know.

Sometimes people feel like they should already know their life purpose. While I think we probably do know somewhere in our being, it's not always a conscious thing. It's like we think we're good communicators because we know how to speak English (or whatever native language we speak), which is not the same thing as being a good communicator. Most people go through life not thinking about living purposefully. They're just going through and following the motions and doing what other people are telling them to do. They're conforming and living between the lines because they don't know there's a different way or that they have options.

In any case, most people start out not having a clear sense of articulated life purpose. The only way to change that is to find tools that work for you to tease it out and give it words. There are times when that life purpose discovery and definition can be so clear you can lock it into everything you're doing—including your business.

Sometimes you'll work through exercises like these and feel like you got nowhere with them. Then, unexpectedly, in a few days or a week or a month, you'll just get a big download—a BOOM—that you know is just "it." Clarity does not always happen on our preferred timing. Insights come when you're ready to see them. Give yourself time to acclimate to these tools and what comes through them. And remember you may get tested for them.

One of my clients was committed to following her life purpose and being self-employed; naturally, this was when she was approached by recruiters offering her dream job of a lifetime. Conversely, another client wanted a job with a regular paycheck, where she could limit her responsibilities to one area of a business when—BOOM—client after client showed up at her door. Suddenly, she was an accidental entrepreneur. However, once you get over the hump of the transition and new opportunities aligned with your purpose open up, things will smooth out in ways you cannot even predict before they happen.

If you've always been employed, there are a few things that need to happen. First, there's a mindset that has to shift from depending on others for a paycheck to depending on your business as a path to prosperity. You start creating your own economy. Your free will and choices determine your experience and your abundance. You're no longer working by a standard 9–5 clock but by what works for you and your clients. When you are not able to make that mindset shift, you get distracted by personal projects, it feels disconcerting, you still work a 9–5 schedule . . . there's a different compulsion because you don't know how to do it differently or don't allow yourself the freedom your business needs you to experience for optimal productivity.

I do believe some people don't know how to focus themselves as an entrepreneur and don't really 'get' that they are accountable for their own results. Entrepreneuring means you get it all—the recognition, the money, the clients . . . but you get the harder times too. Choosing your personal prosperity path takes courage and clarity. And there are not many shortcuts that work out seamlessly in the end.

Hopefully the information here helps minimize that learning curve and maximize your clarity, resources, and opportunities.

All in all, pay attention to what moves you forward and what holds you back. Look at where your time can be better served by doing something different and be scrupulous in your time management. Your life / path / purpose is at stake.

Fear, Resistance, and Doubt

Let's move on to talk about fear, resistance, and doubt because these are the big whoppers that can really bite when you're up against your limitations. Fear is one of the most challenging blocks in achieving entrepreneurial success. The good news is there's a lot you can do to overcome, minimize, or even eliminate fear. More good news is that fear only shows up when you're in action. (If you're not doing anything different, everything stays status quo, known, and comfortable.)

Fear is the great human equalizer because we all experience it. It doesn't matter what your economic status is or age or relationship or health or whatever—fear does not limit itself to expressing the same way for everybody. Everybody fears something, whether it's spiders or the dark or not making enough money to cover the bills this month or whatever. The difference between people who use the fear to help them and those who surrender to it is the ability to focus the fear. When you can recognize fear as a guide to your next best level and then take action in spite of it, you win. Fears can only show up when you're doing something beyond your comfort zone; otherwise there's no reason for those fears to come out of hiding. In a way, that's reassuring because your life flow is moving you to a new experience.

There's a magic in having fear. When you're afraid of getting or having some new result or outcome, or you don't know what you want, the Universe cannot bring it to you. Having clarity around what you want and what you know you can have is another strategy to help handle some of that fear. It's about trusting yourself in your discernment about what's going to actually hurt you or not. So you have to trust yourself and the Universe to bring in your desires, your prosperity, and your next best level.

Some say fear is False Evidence Appearing Real. It can also be Face Everything And Rise. Your perception is what will determine your outcome. Fear is a natural reaction to circumstances. It's instinctual programming that alerts you to and protects you from potential injury, from harm, from things that could have dire consequences.

Our greatest human fear used to be death by saber-toothed tiger; now the greatest fears are little emotional deaths from other kinds of sources—judgment, humiliation, failure. These are intangible, emotional experiences where we feel vulnerable. There's an awareness about where we think we might get emotionally hurt or financially compromised or energetically damaged . . . or it might be about our pride or reputation getting tarnished. The fear might be of being slandered or someone gossiping or getting a negative review. These scenarios are scarier today than facing the likelihood of death by saber-toothed tiger.

When overriding fear, you're going up against an instinctual biological program that's simply trying to keep everything safe and copacetic. Your biological system is geared to make sure you're safe. Fear gets your whole system going and it can either steal your energy away or it can motivate you to take swift and immediate action with the adrenaline it generates throughout the body.

Resistance is a little different from fear in that resistance is confusion. You find resistance where there is self-sabotage or find other people are sabotaging you, which, of course, doesn't happen. It is not possible for others to sabotage you without some level of permission or acquiescence on your part. In other words, nobody else can sabotage you without you allowing it OR unless you use other people as an excuse to sabotage yourself. For example, you might cook a full dinner (aka, self-sabotage of time toward a different goal) because you believe your partner will be upset or disappointed in a frozen pizza or takeout meal when there's a good chance your partner will understand less time spent in meal prep.

Saboteurs are a manifestation of your resistance because whatever's happening 'out there' is a reflection of what's 'in here.' It's not about the out there—there's something within you creating that source of sabotage, which is resistance. Resistance might look like distractions, blaming, focusing on what's external, staying busy—anything that isn't the thing you don't want to address. Resistance generally doesn't feel good, even when you're not looking at it and trying to stay in a pleasant, distracted place. When you see you have some sort of resistance, it's an indicator toward what's next for you.

In the case of the previously mentioned potter, she was going to do a show but was limited to bringing only six pieces. So if she sold them, then what? Naturally, there would be another household family issue where there is suddenly no budget for supplies. She wouldn't have time for artistic creativity. Or she wouldn't find the supplies needed in time. There was limitation echoing throughout her world, including with her friends who were urging her to charge less for her fine art. Her friends—who loved / cared for her—were the ones giving her the message of limitation. These are the people who would most want her to live expansively and, yet, they were the ones (unexpectedly) sharing the message of scarcity. So it's not the exact scenarios that caused her issue; instead, those situations were symptoms of the greater issue in her energy field around limitations.

When you have resistance, it is actually something that needs healing, balancing, addressing with a little TLC (tender loving care).

Resistance can be your best guide to what's possible for you. However, it requires being candid with your interpretations to see what you associate with your source of resistance, your willingness to go beyond the familiar, and your commitment to step into your next purposeful and prosperous level. Hint: it will not likely be what you can see on the surface.

As for doubt, that is the gateway to clarity. When you have doubt, you're questioning something or you have that 'not-knowing' feeling—which is exactly what gets you to clarity. You only have doubt when something needs to be sorted out. Where there is no doubt, you have clarity. This is, once again, where the not-knowing feeling is a jumping off place to new possibilities. Getting comfortable with the not-knowing feeling allows for a lot more energy to move—you're no longer constricted, limited, or controlled by what you already know. Growth always means discomfort. You don't grow when you are comfortable. Instead, you (and everybody else) will tend to coast because you're always looking for safety and having things be copacetic. So your growing edge is when you go beyond anything you know or are familiar with, through discomfort, to a new experience. And doubt signals that you are on a growing edge.

Saboteurs Are Messengers

Resentment, fear, resistance, and saboteurs are messengers to help you get to your next best level sooner than later. They hold focus that your present life isn't the life you were meant to be living. They can set into motion all kinds of consequences, both visible and intangible. When using your mind's eye for vision, keep in your imagination the decision or result you are being guided to create and experience.

There are two ways to consider that scenario. There's the result of where you see yourself going in your experience. There's also one you can create for yourself that keeps you detached from your present life and unable to be productive.

Living in a fantasy place around what you're doing is not helping you to actually create it. There is a pervasive belief that people's highest potential—their purpose—is not who they are now, nor what they're doing now, as though their purpose is not who they see in the mirror every morning. There is a distortion that one's highest potential means some type of ideal life, of something of greater spiritual significance, which is the hook to discovering our innate purpose. We might think our purpose is the secret route that can lead us from the boredom of the mundane everyday world to some magical and enchanted place where all our cares and woes would vanish and we would sparkle as our highest potential automatically shone throughout the lands. This is just not true. Even when you're living on purpose, your laundry still needs to get done.

But the compelling drive toward living our purpose, knowing that inner potential is waiting and wanting to emerge, can relentlessly cause us to create the ideal life as opposed to whatever unhappy situation that is our present life. All this is to say that identifying and expressing your purpose is not an escape hatch to living an amazing life versus what 'is' now.

When you are unhappy and feel you have a greater purpose than what you're living, you can apply that energy with focus into changing your life for the better. The world of imagination is not a place for permanent residence. When the world of imagination makes your physical world painful by the high contrast, be open to guidance from unexpected places. This means going to the not-knowing place and being willing to be vulnerable, which can challenge your ego. Only by being willing to walk the path of such an initiation can you experience a fresh perspective.

Now, when you open to the unknown, you cannot choose how or

when it will show up. Your only option is to welcome or reject it—to say yes or no. Rumi said whether you say yes or no, the consequences of your choice will play out in the seen or unseen universe of your life. Respond with fear of humiliation and you have unleashed your fate; respond with courage and you have opened your highest potential and your destiny.

Allow your saboteurs to guide you to and through opportunities.

Fears of Living Your Wisdom

Let's consider now the most common fears of living your wisdom. When living and working based on your wisdom, it is not necessarily always easy, especially when the people around you may not be living their purpose or from their wisdom. "Stuff" is going to come up. And fear can mask as different things, from anger or impatience to blame, guilt, shame, or any other number of is labeled as 'negative' emotions. We're conditioned to see these emotions as socially unacceptable, so we will tend to deny, stuff, or repress those emotions we judge as negative instead of using the generative power of what they're trying to tell us.

For example, anger can be generative in giving you urgency when running across a busy street. Generative anger does not need to be at a specific thing—it's a momentary response to move you quickly. It can save your life in the right circumstances. Another way to see anger is as a mask for a personal boundary that has been breached. Honoring your boundaries is vital for a quality life. Every emotion we are socialized to judge as negative does have at least one positive application. In many, if not most cases, these powerful emotions are messengers to help you grow.

Fear actually comes from the ego's needs not being met. No one else can actually meet your needs, but it's hard to remember that when fear is present. Even more, when you are activated with a shenpa response running, you may not know what is actually happening because you are no longer conscious in the present at that point.

9 Common Fears of Living Your Life Purpose

Following are the nine most common fears of living your life purpose. There are ways to handle these fears; however, you must first acknowledge they exist.

One: the fear of being rejected and not belonging—being abandoned or being alone or misunderstood.

Being rejected is significant because our number one need is to belong in community. I think that is a safety response because the lone animal outside the herd is usually the target for predators. If you feel like living on purpose might cause you to be rejected or live outside any community, you will likely be afraid to live your life purpose. In the end, fear makes you stronger but, when you're in it, it can be destabilizing and overwhelming.

Two: the fear of making a mistake.

In fact, you might be so afraid of being not perfect that you just don't do anything. Some call this condition 'analysis paralysis.'

Three: the fear of being ridiculed, mocked, or criticized as a "target for bad things to happen" when you live on purpose.

Being a target is not a comfortable place to be…celebrities deal with this kind of visibility and look at what happens to them in the media. Your purpose may make you more visible. People can make fun of you—Donald Trump is a prime example. He is a known public figure and one of the most powerful men in the world at this point; yet, people comment on his hair or complexion. His hair or other superficial observations are how people can relate to him as a person. Being more visible is a double-edged sword.

Four: you may feel like your purpose is too big to do or that you're not enough to do it.

A very public example of this is someone like Oprah, who started her career as a journalist, then a talk show host for what some might call 'superficial' topics. Over time, she has evolved into the emotional guide for generations of fans and audiences around the world. She is a philanthropist, a visionary, a media mogul . . . and, when asked, she says she knew she was special at a young age but did not have any idea that she could become an influencer and household name for the ages.

Five: the fear of the unknown.

You don't know what will happen or how to do it, or where it's going to go or where your purpose will take you. The fear of the unknown can be paralyzing. That is the great power of fear—it can stop you from taking action while you're trying to suss out what's actually happening or take new action.

Six: the fear of living your purpose.

If you don't believe in yourself, if you judge yourself for being who you are, or if you have a vision in your head you need to match and you're not quite there, these thoughts can stop you from moving forward with your life purpose.

Seven: the fear of what others will say.

This fear can cause you to seek validation rather than acting on what you know for yourself.

Eight: the fear of all the 'what ifs'... what if you are living your life purpose but you're not happy?

What if it doesn't feel like you thought it would? What if you don't have excuses to fall back on anymore? All the 'what ifs' come from a future place versus in the present. So all the 'what ifs' are projections. Fear is a lot of distortion, misidentification of what's happening, and duplicated imprints of socialized responses. They dictate how we act vs. feeling empowered to act by what you know despite circumstances. Fear will dictate your actions by default instead of being in that present moment of intelligence.

Nine: the fear of thinking it has already been done.

When you feel your purpose has already been expressed fully by someone else, it is an indicator of low self-worth. Why? Because nobody else can live your purpose the same way you do. You are unique in your experiences, perspective, and natural talent. Clearly the Universe needs you to express that because you have it to offer.

It is possible to inherit a life purpose. You'll know that's the case when something external affects you deeply, especially when it is about family obligations or carrying on a tradition. If something external is influencing what you're doing and how you're doing it, it could be an inherited life purpose.

These fears each invite a level of personal healing. An interesting definition of healing is that it is the erosion of long-established patterns. When there is an erosion of patterns you've known for a really long time and had gotten comfortable with, you might experience dread around what could happen next. That feeling is a messenger of growth—energy is moving in that area again but it's unfamiliar so it feels strange.

I Thought There Would Be More

Here is an exercise to help tease out your purpose from among the fears. It's the "I thought there would be more" idea. That is, when you reach what you thought would be success for you, like having your prosperous business, taking your dream trip, buying your home, or getting married, but...it feels flat, empty, or not what you expected at all, it's the I-thought-there-would-be-more feeling. You finally achieved that idea of success but it doesn't feel like you thought it would . . . which means some aspect of your life purpose is compromised.

You can discover that aspect by taking three minutes or so to fill in the blanks on the following statements. "I thought life after _____ (event) would be more _____ (fill in the blank)." "I thought life would be less _____ (fill in the blank). You want to explore both sides of success to learn about your purpose and any hidden definitions of success.

By stating where you thought your life would be different, you can tease out where it's off-purpose through opposition. That is, you may not know exactly what it should be but you know what it would not be when you achieve it.

You can use variety in these statements as well. "I thought the world would be more / less..." "I thought I would be more / less.. ." "I thought we would be more / less..." "I thought there would be more / less of..." If you can, consider where you most likely formulated these ideas either by age or circumstance.

I remember hanging with my two girlfriends as young 'tweens in the front yard with the picket fence, talking about what our lives would be like when we were really old—like 30. I could never see my future but my friends were on it. One was going to be married with children. The other was moving to New York to have an exotic and amazing life. And all I got was fog. It was challenging and disheartening for me. Yet, because I had no fixed visions, I had no other option than to trust I would be in the right place when I needed to be there. Throughout our lives, each of us experienced exactly what we imagined. Your purpose is always available to you, even when you don't know what it should look like or exactly how to do it.

A quick reminder: I've found that if a person ties their life purpose to making money, it becomes very elusive (both the purpose and the money). Your purpose is the compass that guides you to your prosperity path but it on its own may be showing you the how and not the what.

Tips to Address Fears of Living on Purpose

For our purposes here, let's continue exploring with your divinely inspired purpose as well as tips on how to handle living it. Once you have a sense of your purpose, how will your life reflect that purpose? What changes can you see yourself making as a result? How will your life reveal the purpose you can see beyond the fears, which can come up to block you from taking action? Being purposeful, including with regard to your prosperity path, is about mastering life, decision-making skills, tools, and perspective. You are going further than you have up until this point in your life about understanding and living your purpose because now you're going to be doing it with conscious awareness. Your purpose is the reason behind everything you do. It gives a shape and a form to everything in your life.

A good visual to describe that concept of shape and form is water. Water is purposeful but it needs to have a shape to take form. It's one of the most powerful forces on earth but it needs something outside of itself to hold it, to give it shape and form. The same is true for your life purpose—you get to choose how to express your life purpose. For example, if your purpose is to teach, you will do that whether you're in a corporate position, a stay at home parent, or traipsing the globe having adventures.

It's important you have positive self-esteem, resilience, and trust in both the bigger picture and yourself to live from your purpose. Following are tips you can use to address the fears that *will* come up as you live your purpose.

One way to address the fear is to find positive reactions to hold on to, like savoring your accomplishments, relishing what you've done, and celebrating the new. Then in those moments when you feel that not-knowing feeling, you can remember you have felt that not-knowing before and it turned out great in the end. In general, we don't celebrate our accomplishments enough—daily life can be too busy to take the 'extra' time. There are cultures that ritualize all kinds of life transitions and achievements; we in the western world are not taught the importance of rituals.

A second useful tip is to know yourself and your truth. The truth of others may not be your truth or even the truth. As a result, you need to know what you know, know yourself and your truth because fear fades in the presence of truth. Separate yourself, your identity, and your worth from what you're doing.

Again, in the western world, we are socialized to identify our being-ness with our careers or what we can do for others. When someone asks an ice-breaker question about who you are, how often do you respond with an explanation about your work? (Or the question posed is, 'what do you do?') When you can separate yourself, your identity, and your worth from what you're doing and just be comfortable in your being, fear cannot get a foothold. There's no need to justify who you are or what you're doing, so success doesn't have to look like any preconceived idea which removes the fuel fear needs to exist.

As much as possible, set your intention for what you want, then release the attachment to it showing up in a particular way. For example, if you are so busy looking for long-stemmed roses in a rectangle box, you might miss the beautiful wildflower bouquet in the octagon box—you're too busy looking for what isn't based on your mental projection. If you want to do a joint venture in business in a particular way and someone knocks at your door to ask you to do a public speaking gig, you may not recognize that speaking gig as that JV opportunity. In business, and in life, feel the fear and take inspired action anyway. Stay open to receiving the experience.

Living your life purpose doesn't happen all at once—it's a series of small steps. Simply remove the blocks as you see them, take one step at a time and practice it as you go. While the goal is to live consistently from your purpose, life can get in the way. It can be helpful to take these small steps with good company—like-spirited people who understand and can support you in your journey. They can help remind you of your purpose.

Another tip is to speak your truth. Hold on to your integrity and share what feels right through your communications. When you are speaking your truth, you are sharing light; the only way to know light is to be present to darkness. In this case, darkness means others who don't understand what you're doing through your purpose or enduring repercussions for speaking your truth. The fear of living your purpose by speaking your truth is that relationships will judge or abandon you. This is related to something called the Imposter Phenomenon.

The Imposter Phenomenon is a fear-based condition where you might be seen as successful but you feel that if people really got to know you, they would discover you are an imposter in that success. They would discover you don't really know what you're talking about or don't really deserve XYZ award. This destructive mindframe can be countered with speaking your truth. You are in charge of what you're creating in your life and business and how you're channeling your purpose into presence and action. There's no need for you to have fear because you're the one creating (or co-creating with Source, depending on your beliefs). You are in charge, knowing and living from your truth, so you don't have to experience fear.

It's important to find something to feel joy about in your purpose because fear and joy can't coexist. You can't be in two emotional states at the same time—either you feel joy or you feel fear but not both simultaneously. Now, if you do feel stuck, just break state with that emotional place. Meaning, break up your focus—have a conversation with someone, tell the story of dreams come true to someone who can reflect it back to you, write out the magic in your message in a journal, reframe what's happening in a way that acknowledges the growth opportunity. You're probably seeing the pattern here . . . do something different—stand up, dance, play music, take some action to get out of the glitch of stuck-ness. Then return to the question, challenge or opportunity later with a fresh perspective.

A good question to ask yourself is: how do I diminish myself? In what ways am I marginalizing my value (my light, my life, my relationships, etc.) right now? Your answer is a sign of where you're living out of alignment with your true purpose.

Another good self-question is: who am I trying to please right now—myself or someone else? It can be fascinating to do a quick check on this by reviewing the decisions you've made just in the last month to see if you're choosing because of someone or something else, like fear or conditioned responses, or allowing someone else to make decisions for you.

Once you see the results of your decisions with your newfound clarity, how do you feel about that? Is that your parent's voice in your head? If it's the voice of someone who is no longer in your life, they can still have power in how you're living and who you are being. In these cases, you aren't living on purpose because your purpose is about living in harmony with your own nature vs. someone else's. If it doesn't feel good, it probably isn't good for you. The more you evolve into your purpose, the more your life and business works—your purpose evolves you and its expression evolves with you.

Here is another interesting exercise you can try to tease out your fears around living from your purpose. Imagine friends, colleagues, or family members—people you know—are talking about you when you're not there. It would be as though they don't know you're around and you walk in on them talking. What is the worst thing you could hear about yourself? Finish the phrase: 'The worst thing some-one could say about me is _____.' Once you have that answer, you discover your soft spot for where you might be unconscious, not using your wisdom, or not in alignment with your life purpose. Your goal is to find the word that gets to the center of that—the really vul-nerable place—so you can deliberately course-correct.

For an example, let's say the worst thing someone could say about you is that you are irreverent. Consider the opposite, which is something like respectful. What might be getting short-changed as a result of you being afraid to be seen in a certain way—in this case, as irreverent? The next natural question is: 'what would the quality that may be missing look like, such as being respectful (to use the example above)? And is it one you want to embody? The idea is to find the quality you might have that isn't getting the response or understanding you want from others, as well as to find the quality you want to express more so you can act accordingly. By understanding how you think others perceive you, you can choose to shift how you are showing up through the mental exercise of opposition. And then to determine what the quality of "X", whatever that is, would look like if you were actually incorporating it in your life. (Whew!)

Another exercise is to do the opposite of whatever it is you've been doing. For example, maybe you have been saving a lot of money and cutting back on expenses—in this case, start spending some money for a day or two. Maybe it's like what dieters think of as a 'cheat day.' If you've been holding back on being visible to the world, turn around and make ten phone calls to initiate conversations with people. Basically, see what you're doing, do the opposite, then see how it feels so you can be your own mirror. Mirrors reflect things back to us with a different perspective . . . be your own mirror by doing the opposite of your usual to find your growing edge.

Another potentially insightful exercise is to write out a list of your fears—as many as you can in ten minutes, especially the ones that really freak you out. Once you have them identified, use 'they' to represent how the fears limit you. For example, they don't let me pay my bills easily. Then change it to" 'some part of me doesn't let me pay my bills easily.' Then change it to: 'some of the time, some part of me doesn't let me pay my bills easily.' As you repeat these statements, they will get smaller and more manageable. First, it's an overwhelming fear, which becomes some part of you, which becomes some part of you some of the time . . . which gives context to the fear. That means you can choose to do something to address it. Additionally, by acknowledging the fear and its effects in limiting you, it becomes known . . . and, typically, things in the light are a lot less scary than those same things are in the dark. You will likely find the fears are more manageable and you have more energy to take positive action about it because it's not holding you hostage anymore.

Vulnerabilities That Can Come Up

One of my clients asked the people in her inner circle to help her see any deficiencies she could strengthen in herself. In doing so, when she asked for their reflections, she got lots of positive strengths and found people reluctant to give her any weaknesses. Then, when one person did, she got upset and that surprised her because it was not a serious criticism. She did some inner work to go underneath those feelings to find where she couldn't embrace that insight, since the person delivered the description in a loving way and it wasn't anything awful. That was both the vulnerability and the growth experience for her. She got to explore her inner perfectionist who discounted the 99% of positive feedback to focus on the one area that showed she might not be so perfect. She learned she typically drives herself pretty hard toward reaching a standard, which she thought was normal. She discovered it was nearly impossible to reach the standard of perfection. And therein lies a common vulnerability.

Perfectionists have 'all or nothing' thinking, and are critical of themselves and others. They tend to be pushed toward a goal by a fear of not reaching it and see anything less than a perfect achievement as a total failure. Naturally, being a perfectionist completely clashes with being an entrepreneur because being an entrepreneur means taking calculated risks, doing stuff you don't know how to do, making mistakes, moving forward, learning as you go, and sometimes doing it by the seat of your pants. As a result, while on your prosperity path, it is vital to be aware of and contain or even neutralize your inner perfectionist.

It can be interesting to see where your inner perfectionist 'glitches' on things, like addressing a new challenge or opportunity, because it may or may not be real—other people's judgment can get mixed into your perception. There is the other person's truth, our truth, and then the truth. When something stings, pings, or has a 'charge' to it, there is an opportunity to shine light on a hidden truth or trauma. Essentially, that reaction means it has been brought to your awareness so you have the opportunity to address it. You don't have to let it sit there and affect your energy space or distort your results through aiming for perfection.

In travelling beyond the edge of familiarity in self-insight, one of my clients contemplated her overall life journey. Her intention was to learn what she should focus on to realize her optimal prosperity path. In doing so, she went into a place of not-knowing and realized she was just now awakening to realize where she had been in life. It was disturbing to think she didn't know what she thought she did. Being in not-knowing led to confusion and she couldn't seem to get anything done on her to-do list. She began to consider questions like. . . . How can being in not-knowing create a space or opening to the next level? Does being in confusion equate to not-knowing? And is this like an anteroom, waiting room or some kind of processing station that precedes moving into the next level?

The not-knowing feeling can show up as confusion, or scarcity, or even panic. It shows up in different ways. "I just don't know how I'm gonna do that." "I don't know how I'm gonna pay for that." "I don't know who's going to help me with that." That not-knowing can feel really destabilizing and unsettling. But when you look underneath and let go of the need to know what to expect, then anything that comes in to help you is going to be full of possibility. There's a lot of potent possibility, which is how not-knowing creates space for your new next level.

Let's say you don't know how you are going to pay your bills this month so you decide to create a possibility of trusting the Universe to take care of that. You commit to taking one step at a time. You commit to doing what you know how to do. You commit to putting yourself out there with new opportunities or relationships as they show up. You commit to following through on the next step as it presents.

Those types of mental commitments actually start you in fresh motion when you can look underneath what feels like confusion or panic to doing the next thing as it shows up for you. If you can get past that surface symptom of not breathing, panicking, or beating yourself up for not doing your to-do list, you can become open to what the Universe is trying to bring you.

We entrepreneurs tend to have' bright shiny object syndrome' so we can find ourselves bouncing around with a never-ending to-do list. It becomes vitally important to know priorities and what pulls progress forward. The to-do list can be the greatest nemesis, or best friend. It can be helpful to write down everything in your head on one big sheet of paper. From that, you can prioritize what you want or need to get done. Then you can schedule future items from that list in your calendar so you can cross them off the list for today, knowing they will get attention when the timing is right. That means you are working on two to-do lists to reach your purposeful prosperity—one for today and one for the future.

Out of today's priority list, you can then sort them into three categories: 1) those that are due today, 2) those you can knock out quickly, and, 3) those that need additional information from someone via a quick email request. Send those email requests first, then knock out the easy ones, then make sure to get the bigger, more complex ones done after that. It's really satisfying to cross done items off your big sheet checklist as you work through the list.

Some days you may be ready to just dig in and get the big stuff done because maybe that has the most bang for the buck—in that case, do it and circle back to pick up the low-hanging fruit. The advantage to that is using your personal energy rhythms to maximize your results; morning people have more energy in the morning for bigger projects while night owls feel it's easier and more productive to work after the traditional work day is complete. Know yourself and work accordingly as another purpose alignment strategy.

Other people will have different systems. For example, at the end of a given day, Richard Branson writes his list of the top three things he wants to get done the next day. The next morning when he starts working, he focuses exclusively on those three things until they are done. That means, no voicemail or email or meetings until he gets his top three priorities done.

At any rate, the not-knowing feeling can lead to unexpected outcomes because you don't have a frame of familiar reference. When it comes up, you have to go beyond where you've been, which is outside of your comfort zone. At the same time, when you can settle into that knowing you're going for a ride, you allow the possibility of new outcomes. The feeling of fear and the feeling of excitement are physiologically the same—it's only interpretation that makes it one way or the other. You are always at choice about how to interpret your experience.

The Positive Charge of Living Purposefully

People work really hard and then can't, or don't know how to, live prosperously. Ironically, there is a positive charge (a sting, a ping, shock or jolt, a reaction, an energy surge) that comes from experiencing prosperity and living on purpose. It's like when someone says something like, "you're so much taller in video." A charge is like a little kick or surge of emotional voltage that fritzes your system for a split second. In this case, it's the experience of your response when you have unexpectedly easy abundance.

What would you say if someone walked up and just dropped $100,000 in your lap? Most people would wonder where it came from, who it really belongs to . . . they might even push it away and say it wasn't theirs . . . or not want it because of the perceived pressure to change that would come along with it. When you have a lot of money, are you supposed to be different—dress better? Have a nicer house? Can you keep your same friends or will you have to get new ones? Maybe you aren't sure how to be smart with it . . . how to invest it . . . how to hire the right financial advisor. That knee-jerk initial reaction is the charge that comes with an unexpected, even if positive, event. And instinctively rejecting that $100,000 comes from not knowing how to receive abundance and live prosperously.

The same thing will happen when you're living on purpose without distraction, without the "noise," without worrying about others' opinions, projections, and judgment. When you are going against the norm by living on purpose without defending or justifying it, how will your life change? It might mean you have to let go of friends as you push the edges of their comfort zones. You might have to give up those habits that aren't supporting you. What else might you have to give up?

One of my clients realized that, for her to move forward, she had to release some toxic family relationships. Her family members did not support her positive momentum. She had to break the social context of her life to live on purpose. She had to risk intimidating people in her life as she moved beyond the box where she lived in their head. She had to acknowledge her circle may feel she rejected them simply because she chose to move on and do what was needed for her own alignment with purpose. She had to do this without having a guarantee of how it would turn out or who would be left standing in her life when she did it. While all of this release felt destabilizing, she discovered huge rewards when she made the leap to her next level. When she let go of what was, her business took off nearly overnight. Her self-care improved dramatically with healthy habits and reciprocal relationships. And she felt a deeper peace within herself than she'd ever experienced before.

Living on purpose will require you to have a solid sense of what I call 'havingness'—the ability to actually have and enjoy the results of your work. When you cannot receive or enjoy what you create, that is another facet of a positive charge to your success. In practical terms, it could look like giving to others whatever exceeds your inner 'set point' for prosperity (which feels different from sharing your abundance) or even sabotaging your ability to receive it in the first place. Clients have shared with me their big visions and, when they begin to manifest, back down on it because they need to stretch their mind to actually have what they said they wanted.

My thought on that is we are conditioned to strive and work hard but, too often, we are not prepared for enjoying the benefits of it. We can climb the mountain but don't know where to go once we reach the summit so we slide back down as a return to our familiar way of being—working and striving.

The only solution I can offer on this one is that the next time you receive prosperity in any form and from any source, simply give thanks and enjoy it.

Charting Your Prosperity Path

Now that you know your purpose and, ideally, what you want to share with customers, it's time to operationalize that into your prosperity path. A key aspect of that is to have a business model. A business model means you have packaged what you do in a way that others can consume and find valuable in solving a problem or meeting a need. A business model identifies what you will sell and, therefore, how you will be paid; in other words, it is your prosperity path.

To have a good business model means you must know four critical knowledge factors as follows.

1. **Clarity.** The more clarity you have, the more clarity your business has in terms of business model, ideal customer, and next action steps for growth.

2. **Product.** You must know what you are selling, for how much, and why it matters to your ideal future customers. In operational terms, you must have product development and delivery strategies and priorities.

3. **Marketing strategy.** Marketing is your 'attraction factor' in both message and visibility. It is where sales start . . . the role of a salesperson is to answer questions that personalize the solution and formalize the agreement. Marketing positions your solution with your ideal future customers.

4. **Customer journey.** You must determine how your customer audience will get the most value from your work by creating a customer journey through calls to action (which means giving them options to learn about your work and then to work with you).

Your wisdom is the vehicle for your success; determining how to direct it is your prosperity path. In short, the way to prosperity for you is through doing the thing that comes the easiest to you. That is, if you're a writer, write. If you're a talker, talk. If you're a teacher, teach. The modality with which you are most comfortable will be your smoothest path for creating prosperity from your wisdom.

Choosing A Business Model

That said, the following is a chart with several business models you may want to consider in creating a living from your wisdom. You may find yourself drawn to more than one and/or see where they could combine to support you in making a comfortable living. Be sure to notice how each of the offers builds off the one previous to it for access to you, depth of value to your client(s), and for potential revenues.

Modality	Strengths	Venues	Progressed Business Model
Writer	Uses language and combines words to create compelling action	Book/e-book, reports, guides, email, video scripts, blog	1. Book 2. Autoresponder series for how-to 3. Video product (can be outsourced) 4. Membership site
Teacher	Makes complex concepts attainable	Classes, workshops, seminars, retreats	1. Initial class (tele-/in-person) 2. 4-part class series 3. Workshop 4. Retreat
Speaker	Reaches large numbers of people	Keynote, break-out, speaker bureaus	1. Book (can be outsourced) 2. Speaking gigs 3. elesummit 4. Video product
Actor	Performer who can handle spotlight	Live events, video, stage	1. Intro video series 2. Speak from the stage 3. Workshop 4. Retreat
Coach	Observer who asks the right questions	Phone, Zoom, in-person 1:1 or small groups	1. Intro Teleclass 2. 4-part webinar series 3. Breakthrough session 4. Coaching package

Modality	Strengths	Venues	Progressed Business Model
Mentor	Been there, done that	Phone, Zoom, in-person 1:1 or small groups	1. Intro Video 2. Self-Assessment 3. 1:1 Breakthrough session 4. Mentoring program
Reader	Sees patterns and describes them	Phone, Zoom, in-person 1:1 or small groups	1. Authority blog 2. Local appearances 3. 1:1 session 4. Group classes
Healer	Can hold space with pain	Phone, Zoom, in-person 1:1, group sessions	1. 1:1 sessions 2. Video product 3. Group classes 4. Book
Artist	Translates abstract through creative expression	Physical products, live events, workshops	1. Individual products + interpretation 2. How-to appearances at live events 3. Video product 4. Membership site

Your personal path to prosperity arises naturally from your primary communication preference combined with strategy to deliver value to your ideal clients. Your business model should be something you can put in place to serve both you and your customers with growth potential over time.

(By the way, I've got something later in the book to help you identify your ideal clients. But I digress for now. Read on . . .)

Relationships Create Prosperity

This may seem like a tangent to explore but it's necessary to consider how relationships impact your prosperity path. Relationships are the most direct path to positive personal growth. They are also how you enjoy prosperity because it is others who pay for your work. Whether the relationship is deep or not, sustained over time or merely transactional, every touch point is some level of connection with another person.

Relationships are also mirrors to the degree of self-esteem, self-affinity, and self-confidence you are experiencing. Where you have unhealthy or dysfunctional relationships, you are out of sync with your wisdom. Where you have positive relationships, there is flow. When you have reciprocal relationships in a business context, meaning you deliver value the other pays for, you have a viable prosperity path. The (only) way to earn money in business is through relationships because someone needs to pay for what you are offering—in this case, your wisdom.

Relationships, by definition, require at least one other person to be a relationship. Rigorous relationships often yield the greatest insight. Through interpersonal conflict, you can see where you are not listening to your wisdom. In business, the unhappy customer teaches you where your system is faulty or where your value could be stronger. When you have repetitive patterns of unhappy customers, you will have challenges on your prosperity path.

Without judgment or criticism, be aware of what people reflect back to you. Watch the kinds of conversations you're having and listen to the words people use with you because those are cues and clues about your prosperity path.

There are two observations about that concept. One is that, in a relationship, two people can resist seeing themselves in the mirror of the other. They don't want to go to that place of dealing with the old emotions and clearing out what needs to be cleared by being aware of it. So they play the resistance game and there's a lot of tension and conflict. The other observation is that it quite often shows we need to teach, or we teach, that which we most need to learn. And sometimes our life will take us through this relationship *for* us. That gives us a reflection of all the ways we can get tripped up so that we can teach other people and see those trip-ups that other people go through more easily.

One of the things I've seen with various coaches or courses is that people who are very successful can forget what it was like when they were falling over themselves in trying to become successful. They don't want to talk about when they failed and have come so far on their path that they forget the pitfalls they handled. They want to teach from where they are instead of from where they were in that early moment. When you remember those pitfalls as a solution provider, you naturally have more compassion when helping others. You have greater understanding about how to help those people move forward, rather than trying to push, pull, shove, or even force customers to move in a particular direction.

There is a lot of value in each person's life experiences, including those of your own you would rather forget, regardless of how you judge them. Those experiences may be part of your purpose in teaching you where you're headed. At the same time, we want to portray our success and so adapt a public persona, then believe that we need to live into that current representation instead of our messy and maybe even unattractive truth of experience.

When you find yourself compartmentalizing who you are in different circumstances, you are not heeding your life purpose wisdom. When people are so perfect or have a persona or have attained a certain level of success, they don't want to acknowledge where they've come from…maybe it's because it's so painful that they just want to put it behind them. Whatever the reason, we can never really know the intentions or motivations. We can only look at the behaviors of people and just notice them. We can't ever really know what's happening for people. However, when you are who you are in everything that you're doing and all your relationships, you are congruent no matter the circumstances around you or where you find yourself.

That congruence, self-insight, and self-affinity brings responsibility. When people become really successful and forget that level of responsibility (to extend a hand behind to bring people forward with them), they miss out on a certain kind of joy. The Universe will bring them opportunities to share and give back because, in the end, we are social beings. If they choose not to, it's not "wrong"—but they will have a different experience.

It's important to think about your journey's lowlights as well as the highlights and not judge what you see. Your life doesn't 'just happen' the way it does … there is some part of you creating it out of your purpose and your purpose is working through you. When you don't judge it, you can learn how your purpose works through your life to bring you to your next-level self. Even when things feel like they're falling apart, it could be that disruption was needed for everything to fall into place.

If you do something different than riding with your own flow, you're trying to push the river—and it just doesn't work. You need to go with the flow of who you are to avoid getting stuck or living someone else's expectations. When you have been stuck in patterns for a long time, sometimes even decades, and things start shifting, it can be really unsettling. The natural human tendency is to try to hang on to where we were for safety; however, the message is that the 'known' time is over and now it's about going bigger in some way.

One of my clients had that experience in her mid-fifties. She is an amazing, talented woman with powerhouse credentials on paper, and yet she can't hold on to a job. As a result, she decided she needed to make a complete change and left her last job. She moved to a new city eight hours away where she has some family, but left a relationship and social structure behind. Now she's trying to find a job and she's kind of bouncing around. It's a case of wherever you go, you follow, so she's finding that the more she tries to hold onto the idea of getting a job, the more it's eluding her. She's a thought leader for her industry. While she's playing with the idea of all this, it's really throwing her for a loop and, at the same time, she is visible in the public eye. The situation is giving her the opportunity to do personal healing work. She feels like, until she can get her personal life managed, she cannot possibly step out onto a big public stage.

Many entrepreneurs, especially women, wrestle with that one... it's something like if we're deficient or not living purposefully in one area of life, we believe ourselves incapable of being proficient professionally through our businesses. And yet, your purpose is always revealing itself in some way—regardless of relationships, circumstances, situations, it is always there trying to bring you to your next best level. And challenges, which are different than weaknesses, are your growing edge. In this case, this client finally pushed past her reluctance and went more public with her persona and, as a result, attracted several interviews and new opportunities. After all, it's not about how you look—it's about the energy and substance you deliver.

When aligned and expressing your purpose, your relationships feel more vital, more vibrant. You're attracting the abundance you're aligned with…and abundance goes beyond money, although money is important for living in today's world. But money is just an energy. When you're out of alignment with your own energy, it's hard for things to connect in your world—it's unclear where a particular energy can connect. When you're scattered or fragmented, it's hard to attract what you want because your misalignment creates challenges. You don't know what you'll attract. If you do attract what you want, it won't know where to land—think docking a space shuttle to the space station (one false move means spinning off into space).

However, when you are in integrity with who you are here to be, things that are not for you will just melt away…the things that don't matter, things that block you, things that keep you small. Such circumstances cannot slow you down anymore because you're living from your essence.

So look at relationships that don't feel supportive or reciprocal. Consider where you're spending your time and how you feel about it…where you are spinning your wheels, feel 'less than' afterward, where you are bored or feel stunted are clues to where you have energetic misalignment in relationships. And where you feel light, positive, happy, and optimistic, celebrate! Those are the relationships you want to keep—including with your clients.

Five Elements of Promising and Delivering Value

There are two options when putting your prosperity path together: 1) put your business model together and then fill in the functional venues, or modalities, of promising and delivering value, or 2) consider the elements of promising and delivering value to determine the optimal business model and venues for you and your customers.

1. What and Who.

What are you actually selling? (Hint: it will be some type of or approach to achieving a transformation.) And who is going to get the most benefit from having it? Your answers here form the foundation for everything that happens in your business, from marketing to sales to social media and more.

2. Marketing Strategy.

There are dozens, if not hundreds, of different marketing tactics you can use to promote your business. Your goal is to identify the optimal marketing approach, or strategy, then the best three to five marketing tactics that support that strategy so you can focus your resources appropriately.

3. Relationship Management.

Since all business depends on relationships, even if only from a transactional level, it is important to consider how you will cultivate relationships in a marketing process. You may want to work with a customer relationship management (CRM) program, use a calendar trigger system for touch-base emails or calls, or hire a team to support your follow-through contact processes. Whatever you choose needs to integrate into and be part of your business model.

4. Taste-test Products.

Your future clients need to validate their decision to invest their money with you. The best way to do that is to offer "taste test" products that are low-cost, low-risk, and big-return. For example, you may want to offer a downloadable ebook, checklist, or self-assessment that relates to the solution your work delivers. You could offer a video (one or a series) or webinar. Some business owners offer a free consultation; however, that tactic can suggest you don't value your time in which case others won't either. A paid introductory breakthrough or discovery session may be ideal;

In this scenario, make sure to offer a guarantee which removes the risk for your future client and/or offer a 15-minute meet and greet visit prior to booking the paid session.

5. Product / Service Mix.

It's important to think through the mix of products and services you offer, both to help design the customer journey and to be clear in your upsell process, or progressed business model. There are times when people get really uncomfortable talking about how to progress a client's experience through a business; however, the purpose of thinking through your client's journey is to ensure they get the most value from their investment with you. You want to make sure the value they receive from you is consumable, so they can take it in and apply what they get to achieve the transformation your work promises as well as progress their transformation over time.

When offering services, you only have so many hours in a day; this is the rationale behind group coaching, training, and webinars. By packaging your wisdom into a program, you are delivering tremendous value as a product that can be consumed at your client's convenience.

As a cautionary note, there are a few things you do *not* want to do:

- Keep everything in your head. It's hard to share your projects with potential outsourcers, it can be confusing when all the moving parts start gaining momentum, and you don't have a way to measure progress. By sharing the bigger picture, potential outsourcers can see how their piece fits into the whole picture, which makes it more likely to fit in better.

- Running your business by post-it notes. Every time you jot a note or idea on a scrap of paper, you add to your own confusion. Post-its are great for brainstorming, but at some point those ideas must be organized into a cohesive plan.

- Not delegating effectively. It's vital to have help when building a business so they can handle the things you don't want or are not equipped to do. When you do delegate, make sure you give enough direction to your outsourcers. Let others shine in their areas and you do what only you can do best.

- Working IN vs. ON your business. You are the most valuable player in your business; if you are stuck in day-to-day operations, you cannot get out of your own way enough to be a leader and maintain the strategic perspective needed for growth. By being strategic about business growth, you save time, money, and resources.

Working through all these moving parts that support your prosperity path can seem overwhelming; however, taken one at a time, they will start working together. The key is to pick a beginning and get started.

How to Charge Appropriately

Charging for your work, particularly when it's around your personal services and intellectual property, is challenging for most wisdom workers. It's much easier to price a product than it is to put a value on the transformation you are selling because you need to know and claim your value. Your value is determined through articulating distinctive benefits, and supporting your clients in getting results in a way that couldn't get on their own or elsewhere.

You do want to know what your clients are seeing in the marketplace. I don't believe in 'competition' in the traditional sense; however, it's important to know what factors your clients are using as decision-making criteria and how you measure up to that in the context of your marketplace. Take time to understand other solutions in your area of expertise along with their revenue models. By making yourself a future customer of services similar to yours, you can gain intelligence about how your process and/or results differ from any other providers. As a starting point, look at the higher and lower price points in your market, then identify a high-middle pricing range for your services and products.

There are different revenue models, depending on your business strategy. You can offer a straight fee-for-service / product, which is transactional in nature. You can offer a subscription plan where your clients pay monthly 'dues' to gain access to products and/or services. A retainer is similar in that it offers monthly revenue but it is typically for a higher-end service than what warrants a subscription. You could offer to get paid based on results through a percentage of what's earned, or some combination of the above.

The highest-paid earners in any industry are typically those who have a level of celebrity, so they are being paid for who they are vs. a specific service. If anybody can do what you can do and there is nothing special about you or your approach means that you are replaceable; in other words, you are a commodity. However, when you are a celebrity, you are recognized as unique and having special value. The perception is you are more gifted in your knowledge or can solve problems or remove pain from your clients better than anyone else. To be perceived as an expert means your value to the client is evident through clear and distinctive benefits. You must know what makes you different so you stand out from other providers in your field.

You can reach celebrity status through becoming an industry authority, entertaining your audience, or envisioning the future. For example, which of the following names do you recognize—Karly Pitman, Scott Sandford, or Neil Tyson deGrasse? All three are notable astrophysicists but only one has become a household name. The person with the most 'celebrity' typically gets more of the limelight through tv shows, interviews, and keynote speaking. Once you have celebrity status, your rates become secondary to all other conversations about hiring you or buying your products.

The bottom line is that your value to your clients—your worth—is not what you think it is but, instead, is what your clients determine is appropriate. This is another reason you must know your ideal customer persona intimately so you can speak directly to their problems, your unique benefits they will find most attractive, and what sets you apart from anyone else.

Additionally, not only do you need to charge what you are worth but you also must be able to receive it. One of my clients said she couldn't figure out why she wasn't doing well in her business. She felt comfortable as an expert, had a business name and website, and had practical experience in the field. That all sounded great—until we dug a little deeper. It turned out her clients, up until that point, had all been friends, family, and colleagues from her corporate job. She had never asked for money; even if they tried to pay her, she refused it.

Her business name was distinctive; however, her site was made using a template (as a money-saving tactic) so it was bland. She had no personality in it. Even more, she said that was intentional because she didn't want to overwhelm people with her vivacious personality.

She thought she wouldn't be taken seriously if she expressed her true personality from the beginning of a client relationship. It's easy to see the issues from the outside but, when you're the person having them, it's a different story.

We also discovered she didn't know how to summarize her business with a 30-second 'audio logo' (which some call an elevator pitch). She wasn't charging market rates so even if she did accept money from a client, it was too low and, therefore, was not perceived as credible against the context of the current market.

Some business owners solve this dilemma by working from donations; however, you can't run a business from donations. Donations mean you have a hobby, a non-profit organization, or a gift you share BUT it's not a business. A business means you receive money for the value you provide to your clients within the context of a revenue model.

If you are having thoughts that you are not worth the amount others are charging, then you need to get to the core of why you are not feeling worthy of market-rate fees. When you have limiting beliefs about yourself, such as the popular excuses of: "you aren't worthy / don't deserve it / aren't confident in what you offer", you need to get to the reason you are feeling that way. If you don't deal with this emotion, which is your body's reaction to a thought, which comes from a probably unconscious belief, you will not have a successful business.

When you don't charge appropriately, your rates devalue your professionalism, you're not claiming your value, it puts your client in an awkward situation having to guess at your value and this all supposes that your client can't afford you somehow which reinforces their scarcity consciousness. Remember that people believe they get what they pay for! *And* it's all your money stuff getting in the way anyway, not theirs . . . so you need to understand and articulate your value, charge appropriately, and receive payment for products and services.

You must know you have intrinsic value that is enhanced by creating a business from who you are and the wisdom you can offer in the desire to make a difference in the world. Some of my clients have said they believe when what they do is too easy, it doesn't have value, that it must mean others can do it just as easily. However, the truth is that when something comes easily to you, it's your right path to abundance. Each of us has something we do better than others; our mission is to find out what that is and then, potentially, use it to make a living. People will pay to have their problems solved and their needs met because they have not been able to do it on their own.

Everyone has challenges and wisdom in some way, which sets the stage for what I call 'the sacred exchange' in business. When you can package your unique wisdom in a way that others can easily consume, they get the benefit of your wisdom and the Universe rewards you for sharing it through them when they pay you for it. This is the cycle of wisdom work as a business.

By being your authentic self, living and doing business from your wisdom, you can release self- limiting beliefs and begin to allow all kinds of good fortune into your life. To the degree that you can receive is to the degree that abundance finds you.

Calculate the Real Value of Your Entrepreneurial Time

The following exercise is a way you can calculate how much to charge based on what you want to earn. You'll see first the formula and then an example based on wanting to earn $100,000 / year. Begin by noting your ideal annual income goal as an initial target.

Calculate Your Current Annual Income

Total Income Over Last 3 Months	=	
	x 4 =	
Total Annual Income Based on Current Reality	=	

Example:

Total Income Over Last 3 Months	=	$6,000
	x 4 =	$24,000
Total Annual Income Based on Current Reality	=	$24,000

Calculate Your "Next Step" Income Goal

Your Annual Income Goal	=	
Current Reality (from above)	=	
Current Income Gap (Subtract Goal Less Reality)	=	
	x 10% =	
Current Reality # _____ + Above (Gap # at 10%) _____=		

This is your Next Step Goal—to achieve 10% increase.

Example:

Your Annual Income Goal	=	$100,000
Current Reality (from above)	=	$24,000
Current Income Gap (Subtract Goal Less Reality)	=	$76,000
	x 10% =	$7,600
Current Reality #is $24,000 + Above / Gap is $7,600	=	$31,600

Calculate Your Hourly Income Needed to Meet Your Financial Goal

Your Next Step Goal (from above)	=	
Number of days you want to work weekly?	=	
Number of hours you want to work daily?	=	
25% of that total (so divide by 4)	=	

This is the total number of productive hours you have weekly. (Discovering that your truly productive, revenue-earning time is only 25% of your week can be shocking. Why only 25% each week? Because you have to account for handling administrative tasks, marketing, commuting, customer support, delegation, etc. which do not produce revenue.)

Example:

Your Next Step Goal (from above)	=	$31,600
Number of days you want to work weekly?	=	5
Number of hours you want to work daily?	=	6
25% of that total (so divide by 4)	=	7.5
Number of weeks you want to work each year?	=	50
Productive hours x number of weeks = # of productive hours per year	=	375

Now for the big finale...take your Next Step annual income goal and divide it by the total number of productive hours you will have this year.

Next Step Annual Income Goal / Productive hours	=	
What you MUST make per hour	=	

This is what your time is worth hourly.

Divide by 60 to get your minute rate	/60	=	

This is what your time is worth by the minute.

Example:

Next Step Annual Income Goal / Productive hours		=	$31,600 / 375
What you MUST make per hour		=	$84.27
Divide by 60 to get your minute rate	/60	=	$1.40

This insight can change how much time you spend watching Youtube videos or talking on the phone because every minute means you are sacrificing revenue-producing activities. Now you know exactly how much you are giving away minute by minute.

The Lifetime Value of a Client

One place to begin deepening your understanding of your client relationships is by looking at the value your client offers over their lifetime with you. Following is a formula that shows how valuable each of your clients can be for you.

Average purchase $_____ x # of Purchases / Yr _____
= $ _____ Annual Total

Annual total $_____ x Avg Life Span of Client (in Yrs) _____
= _____ Client Total

Client total $_____ x # of Referrals _____
= $_____ Value of Referrals

Value of referrals $_____ x Client Total $_____
= $ Lifetime Value of Client

If the Lifetime Value of Your Client was something like $10,000, would it be worth it to you to try to keep them? And if yes, wouldn't it make sense to offer supreme service to retain their business?

Here's one of the fastest ways to know that your clients will appreciate and continue to work with you: give your clients what you yourself would like to receive. In other words, it's what you learned as a child—the Golden Rule—applied to business.

You've probably found customer service to be lacking in many businesses, because technology has made it easier for us to communicate but the personal touch is missing. To make sure you don't fall into that trap, make sure to answer your emails within a 48-hour turn-around or less. If you're available, always answer your phone (unless that takes you away from a dedicated project or another client). Be on time for appointments and group events like seminars, teleclasses, and webinars—especially when you are the leader—because that sets an example and lets people know their time is important (as is yours). As you honor others, you are so honored.

Consider what you can do off-line to stay in touch and service your clients. For example, send personal cards (you can use an auto-mated service to do that) or "surprise" thank you gifts. If it's been more than a few months, pick up the phone to call and check in with your client. People appreciate the personal touch and it could lead to new business because it makes it easy for people to refer their friends and family to you. You stay top of mind and current; they have a solu-tion ready to be referred. And be sure to ask for referrals! When you let your clients know you are looking to help more people like them, your clients become your best ambassadors.

Simple service principles can lead to absolute satisfaction in a well-delivered solution *and* create a solid business with predictable rev-enues through customers who continue to work with you over time.

The Only Thing You Need to Know About Sales

In working with clients over the years, the three things that tend to stop them from having a business are: 1) infrastructure, 2) legalities, and 3) sales. All three are relatively simple to solve—hire experts to help with establishing a solid infrastructure and ensuring compliance with the law, and remember that sales are simply about customer service. That is, when you don't sell your work, your would-be cus-tomers do not benefit from it. Their needs will go unmet and their problems will continue because they don't have your solution. Also, infrastructure and legalities are often one-offs that need to be established and then simply serve your business while sales is, obviously, on-going.

The reality is that marketing and sales are on the same continuum in that the 'sale' actually begins with marketing. Marketing is about positioning your solution with your ideal clients to attract their interest so the salesperson can personalize your solution, answer questions, and formalize beginning your new working relationship. Sales do not need high pressure closing tactics; instead, they happen as a result of good marketing.

Another key to remember is that, when selling becomes uncomfortable, it means either ego or attachment to an outcome is involved. When you focus on the message vs. you being the messenger, you are showing up for your future client without ego to clog up the connection.

Another important reminder is to know that any one particular client is not your source, because Source is your source. Meaning that it can be easy to think that if *only* that *one* client would pay up already ...but it's not about that one client. Source always has your back. So it's about trusting the bigger picture vs. thinking that *one* client or project is your source.

When you feel good about the value you can bring to a client, it is a good relationship for both of you. If you have to 'convince,' 'persuade,' or defend your rates with a potential client, that client is either not ready or is not a right fit with you. It is far preferable to release that relationship and go on to work with an ideal client than to try to push for that one client to follow through with you. When you are saying yes to a client who is not an ideal client, you are saying no to your ideal client because you only have so much time to 'sell.' Also, when it is not working out for a client at the moment, you may find they pull their resources together and then come back to work with you when they are ready and it's better timing for their finances. In fact, they may become your best client because they know the value of your work and have faced the challenge of resource-gathering in preparation. Often where a challenge has been conquered, the reward is sweeter.

So be sure to focus your selling conversations on the message (vs. the messenger), the solution being of service, and ensuring it feels good for both of you to continue progressing your relationship.

Remember, money is only an energy—but it is a powerful one. It motivates people to do all kinds of things, from eating crazy things on reality shows to filing fraudulent insurance claims to finding a life partner. It's big. And it's imperative to honor it for the significance it holds while living here on this physical plane.

Whether you are selling transformational services, health products, offering self-improvement or wellness courses, marketing strategies, and/or coaching /consulting services, how you choose to honor the highest good for yourself, your customers and the improvement of the world is the reflection of your integrity as an inspired business owner.

It's not what you're doing in your business but *how* you're doing it—and with whom—that matters. Being responsible for what you are creating in the world is not for the faint of heart. It calls upon courage, compassion, intelligence, honesty, candor, generosity, awareness, understanding, consciousness, and more.

It means making sure you are always taking "the high road," working with your systems to make sure they are "tight" (streamlined, functioning and following industry standards), that your staff is educated and modeling this behavior, that your vendors are providing the best quality, that your selling conversations are about meeting the needs of your customers—and that's just for starters!

Pay attention to the language you use, how you talk to people, your level of presence in conversation and how you treat other people, as well as yourself, to evaluate your ability to handle increasing social responsibility (which will happen as you grow your business).

If you look at the most successful business people in the world—defined not just by finances but also by quality of life, they are balanced, they are fair, and they are role models to emulate. They are socially responsible with the power they have earned. They have worked in a way that aligns with the highest universal energies because it reflects their best self. They have had the commitment it takes to get through the hard times and, likely, have done it with grace.

Selling is not about desperation, manipulation, or forcing a deal; instead, let your purpose guide you to be of sincere service in helping your customer meet their need or solve their problem through your solution. The magic is in the message. And your purpose shared is what leads to your prosperity.

The Secret Behind Opportunities

Our purpose here is to create a formula for making a living based on your wisdom, purposeful expression, and opportunities. Let's explore opportunities... including the following grand irony.

Opportunities Are Everywhere!

Despite the title of this guide, you don't actually need to *make* opportunities—because they are everywhere! Instead, it's about developing discernment to determine which ones are worth your pursuit.

Think of it like driving in traffic when you want to pass someone—how do you know when to pull out? Which "hole" is yours to take? And what happens if you don't take it? Your driving experience and inner wisdom help you to routinely make that decision. You identify your opportunities to pass based on current conditions and what you have previously experienced (aka, a form of wisdom). The same is true of any other opportunity in life and/or business.

An opportunity is an opening to get to your next place, or level, of being. Often an opportunity involves some degree of growth in order to be able to take advantage of and/or sustain it.

And if you have a karmic agreement to grow in a particular area, you will have continuous opportunities appear over your lifetime to help you learn what you need for your next level. Once you "get" whatever it is you needed to learn, you graduate to your next set of opportunities. But you know this… it is part of the wisdom you're actually here to teach.

Three Ways to Identify a Good Opportunity

To be clear, here are three ways to determine a good opportunity:

1. The growth / benefit potential exceeds the required input.

If you can see that the end reward is positive despite the effort and whatever else is needed for you to take advantage of the opportunity, chances are it's a good one for you.

If the magnitude of what is required from you is daunting or overwhelming, but you have even a glimmer of something better as a result of the opportunity, it's worth taking the risk.

After all, it's about experiencing the range of your personal possibilities for your best growth AND to add to your 'wisdom bank' to benefit others over time.

2. It keeps showing up for you.

If it seems that the same types of opportunities keep presenting, such as you are attracting the same difficult client with a different name or your energy fades out at the same time of day or your money issues don't change over time, these are patterns of opportunities that are inviting you to get to your next level. (The only thing worse than this type of opportunity showing up is NOT having it show up for you—or not being able to see it to move forward in a bigger way!)

If you see a pattern to your opportunities, it's time to do something different—take advantage of it and see where it takes you!

3. You will regret not taking it.

There are times when you may not know an opportunity is the right one or at the right time, but you can feel that you would experience loss, sadness, or regret if you don't take advantage of it when it's right there.

Sometimes it comes down to a split decision in the moment—that is your spirit demanding you show up for yourself beyond your comfort zone and in trust that you will have the experience and outcomes you need in your best and highest good.

Ideally, at any point in your life, you can look at where you are and where you've been without regret. Just do it!

In my humble opinion, suffering is at least partially attributable to missed opportunities. We see them in hindsight or are bound by some external "thing" (people's opinions, perceptions of our own lack of resources or whatever) to not see them or not take advantage of them when they show up.

The only solace we can take from that awareness is knowing that we will get another chance if it is truly our opportunity. It will come again, maybe in a different form and at another time but, once you see it on any level, you can know it as your next best opportunity.

Now let's bring all that down to a business level. As an entrepreneur (someone who is offering a valuable deliverable to solve a problem or meet a need in exchange for money), you need to determine which opportunities will benefit you and your business the most. In business, a good opportunity . . .

- Teaches you something you must have for knowledge or experience.

- Brings you one step closer to your goals.

- Generates a return greater than the input(s) required to activate it.

Conscious Decision-Making

Your values help determine how you make decisions. Values are the compass that both filter and interpret the world in practical terms for taking right action. You know what you value through your vision for the future as well as where you invest your time and energy to reach it. For example, when you value family as a priority, you structure your workday accordingly. When you value self-care, you make sure to nourish yourself, get enough rest and water, and take time for breaks throughout the day. Your decisions are based on your values.

Secondarily, when working in concert with the rhythm of your wisdom and being on purpose, you are—by default—going to be making decisions from a conscious place. Your purpose and your wisdom have helped shape your values over time.

When you are following what you know, actively engaged on your growing edge through being a wisdom worker on an intentional prosperity path, you become responsible for what you know and who you become in the process. Your decisions come from the knowingness you can access (through your values, your insights, your purpose). Many people do not want that responsibility so they go through the motions, 'asleep' in the proverbial sense, rather than being accountable to their truth.

To live in alignment with your wisdom, you have to decide on a regular basis if something is what you want it to be, do, or have, and then what will being, or doing or having it do in helping you live in your purpose. Does "it" contribute to your better state of being in the world? Does "it" allow you to share more wisdom with more people in a way that works for you and for your clients? You have to know what you're willing to sacrifice to become that which resonates with your purpose. Along with that, you also have to know what you won't sacrifice to be, have, or do what it is that you want. That's what it means to make a conscious decision.

How does the decision make you feel? You can project out beyond the results you think you'll experience to feel what you think you'll feel. By doing that, you can look for the rough spots, as in whether it's dark, dense, or heavy. Sometimes you can make a conscious decision by considering your future regret(s) or even whether the decision you're making will matter in a week or a month or three months or six or a year or a decade from now. That can help you decide how much energy you're willing to put into it. And it will also help you decide what the cost of resisting that decision will be for you.

Use your mind's eye to look at how it's going to feel or turn out for you over time. Just send yourself out over some degree of time and project where your life or intended result changes. Look to see what happens around that result. What happens if you don't lose the weight and become a size eight again? You might see it in three months and then in a year to see the change point. You can decode what happens at that point. Then you can make a new decision.

Conscious decision-making cannot happen from a place of fear or scarcity or even money. While you do want to be conscious about your money, when decisions are made from fear or scarcity, you are not allowing for pure potential or abundance. It's not coming from an aligned or purposeful place. It's the difference between being pushed to do something or being pulled toward doing something. Your guidance for decisions can come from resentment, frustration, anger, discontent . . . people are more motivated to move away from pain than they are pleasure. But when you're not happy, be prepared to look at what's causing that state of being so you can make informed decisions about how to shift that experience.

Make Your Feng Shui Work For You

As a Feng Shui practitioner for more years than seem possible, I feel I have to share a bit about how your environment reflects your purpose and your prosperity (or not). Your Feng Shui will affect the opportunities that come to you.

Some people think Feng Shui is fancy interior decorating, others describe it as energy work; I say yes to both. Feng Shui is the ancient art and science of working with your environment, which is your external body, to harmonize with your life goals and support your success. There is power in how you program your external body, your environment, for what you want to experience.

It's both fascinating and illuminating to take an inventory of what's happening in your world through the perspective of your environment. Take a look around you right now—what do you see? Do you love everything around you? Do you feel comfortable? Is there anything broken or out of place or that doesn't serve you? Is there clutter? If any of those things are the case, that's a red flag for something that a) has meaning and b) needs attention. Everything that's 'out there' is something you've created or put in that space to be in your world for a particular reason, and which may not be an accurate reflection of your purpose or prosperity path any longer.

For example, files piled on the floor create obstacles that you need to climb to be successful. You are literally creating your own challenges. Why? Because the floor is the foundation from which everything grows so if your 'floor filing system' is activated, you're actually putting obstacles in your own way to block you from moving forward more freely. You may have done that in the past to build strength or stall results until you were ready for them. To change your results, consider the condition of your floor to ensure it is clean, feels open, and is in good shape. This helps you to create space for clarity and fresh traction toward your goals.

When you're sitting at your desk, how do you feel? Is your desk big enough for your needs? If your desk is too small to handle your business, then you're limiting the flow of what can come into your business. The space to handle your business is constricted. I worked with a client who had a basement office where he couldn't stand up straight and was using his kid's cast-off desk to run his real estate business—and, yet, was surprised he didn't have the number of deals he wanted to be processing.

Do you have mementos from people you don't care for or white elephant gifts you don't like? If yes, do they make you laugh or do you want to throw it out the window? If something is just collecting dust, then find it a new home.

There are many different ways to look at the Feng Shui of your world. It's the books you read, the movies you watch . . . it's literally anything in your world whether physical, emotional, intellectual, spiritual, environmental, creative or anything else. If you were a fish, it would be everything in your tank—the water, the oxygen, the filtration system, the gravel, other fish, floating scuba diver, and treasure chest. So your environmental mirror includes what you're doing with your business, your life, your money, your relationships, and even what you know about yourself. Your Feng Shui will show the degree to which you are tuned into your own wisdom.

In considering only your finances, you can see how you're handling your money, how you're spending it, how you're saving it, how you're calling it in . . . essentially, whether you are owning the numbers or not. Do you know what's in your credit report? Do you cultivate positive financial habits to have a good FICO score? This aspect alone will either support or block you in having what you want for larger financial purchases.

If you find that something is overwhelming or doesn't feel good (either in your environment or in your daily activities), say that box of receipts or balancing your checkbook, you can delegate those activities. There are usually ways to get around what doesn't feel good because those are things taking you off your purpose.

Let's consider your public story or what's called your fame and reputation in Feng Shui. What are people talking about when they think of you and your business? Whether you are aware of it or not, you give them words to help them understand the value of what you're doing through your business offers. Do they have kind things to say about you? Do they have accurate things to say about you? Do you feel like you have truth with what's happening in your communications? Clearly your communications and reputation will influence what happens along your prosperity path.

Now it might be painful if you see you're creating something you don't like; in that case, it simply means there's a misalignment somewhere. When you're looking in a particular mirror (money, business, relationships, etc.), remember you created what you already have as a way to empower your creativity. You have the standard of living you now experience because you created it, which means you have the ability to create something new. You can shift what you'll see in your future mirror. The way you do that is to look at the mirror as it is today to identify the misalignments and then see what it is you want to shift as already complete and present in your energy field. Once you have aligned with your vision and have taken action to experience it (which is simple but not easy), there is no other option than for your desire to manifest on the physical plane.

You can also use color as an indicator of how your purpose is expressing itself (or isn't) by simply looking in your closet to see the predominant color(s) of your clothing. One of my clients discovered her closet was full of black and white colors, which are two very powerful colors, especially in combination. It is all about boundaries, a cutting energy, very definitive—literally her world (and how she thought, etc.) was black and white. If you find you have a lot of red in your closet, that's an auspicious color for passion and power. If you have blue, that's about connecting to your inner wisdom and people trusting you. Green is about change, growth, transformation, transition, and money. So pay attention to the predominant colors in your world to learn what energy is present in your life at the moment.

Use a Tolerations List

Another good tool you can work with is a tolerations list. Go around your life and look for things that bug you. What's the stuff you're having to tolerate to get through the day? What are you putting up with that irks you regularly? Maybe it's that your printer paper is underneath all the folders and it makes it hard to refill your printer. Or maybe when you reach for that fresh paper, everything around it falls and makes a mess.

One of my executive clients called me because he said he just felt cranky all the time and couldn't figure out why he was upset in starting his morning every day. Finally we figured out his closet, where he stored his socks, did not have a light in it. He had blue and black socks; when he did laundry, he just threw everything in one drawer and it was all jumbled up. Every morning, he had to fumble around in the dark closet trying to match socks. And it ticked him off...every single morning. Something that small inconvenience was enough to irritate him for the first couple of hours of his day. He was a bit of a clotheshorse and he got to where he just dreaded getting dressed. It took us some time to figure this out but only about five minutes to correct.

So what are the tolerations? What things are you putting up with that could be addressed to improve the quality of your life? What are the things that are causing you to slow down, that have friction, that make things harder for you? Can you easily reach your pens if you need them? Is your mouse and keyboard set up properly for easy access? Does your desk chair feel good? Can you see a clock or out through the window? These are environmental tolerations but, naturally, there are others. Are your relationships fulfilling? Do you need to have an overdue conversation with someone? Is there anyone who you've been meaning to see but it just hasn't worked out? Do you find you send someone emails and they're too busy to answer you?

Whatever your tolerations, you want to make your list and then start working them three at a time. Three is a good number because that's manageable in a day. Address them and then check them off of your list. Maybe it's the squeaky door, or changing the air filters, or cleaning the junk drawer...whatever it is, start addressing those tolerations so your life can get smoother. Those things won't be irking you in the back of your mind.

Now what if your tolerations list is just so overwhelming that the idea of even doing it is too much? Maybe it doesn't seem like it's going to put a dent in it soon enough to make a positive difference? As an entrepreneur, you've always got things running on multiple levels. You're always thinking of all these things all at once while you're multitasking. And you've got multiple responsibilities with family or social life or working out or whatever.

So you've got all this stuff going on all the time, which is the first point—you really do have a lot going on. Secondly, if you can get your list together, even if it is 12 feet long, it's better than just having these tolerations floating around without focus. Your tolerations list will, at the very least, corral everything into one place. By doing that, you may be able to even one at a time or delegate one thing at a time. Small actions taken consistently will add up to big results over time.

I watched a show on hoarders the other night. The professionals would approach working with these hoarders, who were completely overwhelmed by their space, very gently. These hoarders had genuine angst as the professionals were throwing out what looked like trash—they were sweating, and upset, and felt out of control. They had made their stuff have a greater meaning than what was reality. One man didn't want to throw away envelopes that had his mom's name on them, even though they were junk mail, because she had passed five years earlier because he thought trashing them would mean he wasn't honoring her memory. It was the emotional connection to what was there that made it difficult.

The same can hold true for your tolerations list. But you absolutely won't make a dent in it unless you get started somewhere. Plus when you have a list, there are things identified that other people can help you get handled.

The hoarders show would do a follow-up thirty or ninety days later and show how these people had reclaimed their lives. They had a social life again where people could come visit. They felt better physically. Their life was no longer clogged by the clutter. Overwhelm had been their life previously. By getting out of overwhelm, which is a bit like having clogged arteries whether physical or energetic, life can start flowing again.

There is another possibility about your tolerations list in that you may find the things on it don't really bug you as much as you thought they did; in that case, you can cross those things off your list and not think about them again. You can also start crossing off the things you won't get to so you can get it down to what you can focus on for the next 30 days. For example, if you committed to handling one a day, that's 30 things in a month. That's actually a Feng Shui ritual—if you want to create change in your life, move one thing in your house every day for 27 days.

You can also break your to-do list down so it's more delegatable. You can schedule your tasks out. The Kaizen way, a Japanese system for productivity, teaches focus and taking action in increments of just five minutes a day so, over time, you achieve your big goal.

The big takeaway is that you don't need to tolerate anything in your life or business, including in your environment; simply find a way to get it handled whether it's by you or someone else.

Instead, focus on the opportunities and consciously decide which you want to pursue. Then invest yourself into what you need to make the most of them.

Invest In Your Life and Wisdom

One way to begin living through your wisdom, rather than waiting for a vision or clear direction to come through you, is to just start changing what you're frustrated with today. Why? Because that's what you know, and it's what's obvious to create change. Even if it's just changing a pattern of response within you to some situation, by simply stopping it from letting it take away your power can change the alchemy of your entire life in that one choice. That means it doesn't matter if you can't see far into your distant future. Many people have a hard time just being here now. So stop dwelling on the past, especially if it's painful, and invest in your life now.

Your business can only grow as fast as you do. When you evolve yourself, you increase your capacity to grow your business. Because growth happens through relationships, and because experience is the best teacher, investing in working with a professional—a coach, a mentor, a trainer, etc.—can be the fastest path to prosperity through your wisdom work.

There are several reasons for this...

1. You have to get out of your own head—you can't see your own blind spots and, just as light and dark cannot coexist, the energy that creates a problem cannot solve it.

2. You are pioneering a new way of being by breaking tradition with family patterns, going beyond your comfort zones, or even blazing a trail in your industry. That's grounds for treason in many families or communities of people who have known you for a long time. You need support from someone outside that circle.

3. You can get the "shortcut" from someone else—you don't need to go through trials and tribulations to compress your learning curve and create wins faster and easier.

4. You gain focus and optimize your actions for next best steps because someone with experience and a different perspective can guide you along the way.

5. Friends and family are there to love and protect you, which may also keep you from taking the risks needed to go beyond the familiar. More on this a bit later in this chapter.

When you invest in yourself, you are investing in your clarity. Clarity is power. Clarity means staying present with the current moment to allow your purposeful expression of your inner certainty. That means what you do is secondary to how you do it. It's not what happens to you, but how you handle it.

Life tells you what it wants you to do. As it does, you see some form of consciousness your purpose wants you to bring to your slice of life. When you honor the little things, the big things have more clarity and room to come in... being in the presence of your purpose is what allows it to bloom. Can you be in that simple space? Can you sit with the knowing of the significance in the small things? Are you able to allow this moment to be what it is?

Invest your life in your life—that's part of your purpose. When you're in present moments of intelligence, each moment will show you what you should be doing, which simply means having an empowered purpose. You are the presence that allows your purpose to express and grow. There's a simplicity to that. When you focus on being able to allow this moment to be what it is, then you'll know what to do to be in the expression of your purpose.

You can tell when someone's acting out of presence for themselves because they have conditioned responses—mental and superficial. Their presence is not an expression of their true purpose because they're not able to allow that moment for what it is without judging it in some way. They're just not all there; instead, they're reacting to a stimulus with conditioned responses.

Pema Chodron is a Buddhist teacher who teaches a concept called *shenpa,* which means when people are hooked in their story, their past, they are not present in the moment. Shenpa is the emotional trigger that hooks, or hijacks, their experience. When someone is activated and in shenpa, you can almost see them leave their body—their eyes glaze over, their body stiffens a bit, and they're just not 'home' anymore. In that shenpa moment, there is no way to stay in a purposeful place because, whatever that hook is, it's usually so interfaced with a trigger that it is seeking the healing resolution. That healing is why the shenpa response emerged—to get resolution. Shenpa helps move that person to their purposeful clarity. It's important to distinguish that the shenpa itself isn't necessarily a purpose in and of itself. The shenpa is actually the thing that's stuck and in the way—it's a symptom of the impulse toward being on purpose.

Growth Means Leaving the Status Quo

Does present moment intelligence require you to know your purposeful wisdom for it to work? As in, can you not know your wisdom and still allow the moment to be what it is? I say yes because when you have that present moment intelligence, you are on purpose with the wisdom needed in that moment.

The environment for purposeful wisdom is the present because only in the present can we experience what *is*. All is fully in the present now. You have access to knowing everything because the potential is in every moment and is being that present moment intelligence. Allowing that intelligence to flow through is what allows your purposeful wisdom to bloom and express to be for your highest good.

Do you always know exactly what you're supposed to do if you stop and think about it? While we too often give away our power, I would say yes. We say, "I don't know" when we do know the answer in that moment—we simply need to check in to get it with clarity from ourselves and not others. Why don't we do that? It's a socialized response . . . we don't want to risk humiliation by being wrong or too forceful about our own agenda. Not knowing or being too direct is the polite thing to do. It makes others more comfortable and gives them space to step forward with what they don't (or do) know, which we usually think is better than what we know. Knowing requires being able to stop, slow down, breathe, and check in. Your language will also change when you step into your knowing. You might acknowledge you need to stop and tune in to get clarity but, when on purpose and following your wisdom, you know that you will know what you need to know in right timing.

One of the teachings I share with clients when they say they don't know or aren't sure of something is to consider that feeling of uncertainty as a signal they are going beyond what's known, familiar, and expected. They've left their comfort zone and are out of bounds with their status quo territory. When I then ask them what they would say if they *did* know, they somehow gain the ability to open to possibility and state the action they would take as a result of their knowing. They will even go so far as to clarify, "Oh, I wouldn't do it like that—

I would do this." So they do know but they don't know that they know or don't want to admit it in polite company.

You might get caught in that trap as well so you need tools to pull that knowingness out in a new way. By using your logic to ask questions, your intelligence is compelled to answer them. Your logical left brain seeks to know the information your intuitive right brain has access to on multiple levels. To even begin to access your greater potential, you must access your right brain where imagination lives—and not just the fantasy kind. Your right brain knows what is 'right' in the largest, most real, sense.

When you can tune into that intuitive wisdom, you get answers. Some cultures believe intuition is the true source of knowledge. Here in the Western world, we've been socialized and acculturated to believe we need to do things in a linear way. This comes from the industrial age revolution where we found automation and conveyor belts could give us predictable, streamlined results. Somewhere along the line, someone determined that logic was the only way to prove out something was real, that truth has to be provable in a tangible way. Science says the only way we can know what we know is through logic, but the truth is we know without having tangible proof. We can know and live in wisdom, which then creates the result materially.

We are manifestors of the divine in physical form. That's what the Energy Economy and transformation-oriented business is about now, where knowledge workers, intuitives, and emotionally intelligent professionals are creating value through what they know—their wisdom. It's about being conscious of your power through living your purposeful wisdom in robust expression.

In any case, growth always means discomfort because it's going past what you know, expect, and find familiar. It means breaking through the status quo, leaving the comfort zone, and trying something new. Once you experience success through growth, the new environment (aka, status quo) feels natural—until it's time to grow again.

The Truth About Manifesting

Let's consider the truth about manifesting. Manifesting is the act of making real or actualizing a particular intention or outcome. Abraham Hicks says, "... physical humans are saying 'give me the truth, give me the truth.'" And we say there all are all kinds of truths. Choose the truths that serve you. Now there are a lot of people who would feel great discomfort with that. But the thing that we want you to hear about it is this—there is a truth of cancer, and there is a truth of wellness. Which truth serves you? You can activate either of them within you and make it your truth. Truths are created—they aren't static. Truths aren't conditions that exist that then it is your obligation to identify and catalog. You are the creator of your truth and what you are living is your truth."

That quote is rich with teachings in that it addresses the definition of truth *and* how your interpretation of something is the experience you then live. Going further, I interpret those insights to mean you channel your prosperity through your purpose. You get to choose how prosperity flows through your life and the truths with which you align to, ultimately, create your daily choices and lifestyle.

Believing in yourself and owning what you've created so far empowers your ability to create what you want going forward (aka, manifest). If you look around your life and think how unhappy or displeased with it you are, you are disempowering yourself in creating something new. While what you have now may not be what you want, it is also your launch pad for something new. Rather than say you're not a good creator, look around and be grateful about what you've already created as the fuel to create something new going forward. Your vision, your appreciation, and your ability to be open to receiving what comes in is the manifestation process. Don't worry about the 'how' or the form by which things are going to show up—simply watch for your intentions to present. It is inevitable when your focus and energy are aligned and supportive of an outcome.

Humans naturally look to confirm what it is we think we already know; however, in opening a new way to achieve an intention, it is your purpose—not your history—that will lead to your next best step. Instead of confirming what you already know, you can simply be open to whatever happens even when you don't know what that means because your purpose becomes your compass. Your purpose will actually lead to your next best step, resource, relationship, or opportunity. When thinking about manifesting from a place of clarity and alignment with your purpose, things can show up in a whole different way. You can manifest more of what you want and, when you do, it will be in alignment with who you are in your larger being-ness.

What can you reasonably expect as you live your prosperity path with purpose? One of the most noticeable mirrors of your alignment is that people will act differently toward you. Their response will reflect how far out of alignment you've been with your purpose until now. One consequence of stepping into your purpose is that you might lose relationships. You might find things end or break unexpectedly. You might find yourself frustrated, restless or impatient because you want things to go faster or you want people to understand what's happening without judgment.

One of my clients had a self-discovery process that was really intense. As a result, he learned his life purpose and was so excited about it that, when he went back to work at his job, he shared the great news—he knew his purpose and, even more, he wanted to help other people know theirs as well. As he shared, his colleagues basically stopped talking to him because he was upsetting the status quo.

Everyone learns in their own time. Family is usually the last to know about your changes because they may be critical of the 'new' you or may try to guide you back into the person they knew you to be to fit their perceptions of you. As you live into your purpose, you need to expect that your family may not necessarily recognize it as quickly as your friends, or think it's a good thing. And your friends might judge you for it or you might experience some interpersonal conflicts because the vibrational alignment is out of whack. People may not know what it is but the resonance factor, meaning how they experience you on a vibrational level, is a game-changer.

Remember that time is not actually a factor in your purposeful feeling and the expression of it because your purpose is always there. Rather, it's important for you to not judge what is right now in the moment and simply see the possibilities. The essence of your purpose is embodied, felt, and reflected in how you show up. It's not always tangible, but its effects are everywhere. You will start attracting different situations in relationships, opportunities, circumstances, and people. It's amazing how things will start falling into place when you live from your purpose.

Here is an exercise you can use to psychically measure various elements in your life on a scale of one to twelve...I call it the Clock Face. In your mind's eye, see a one-handed clock face, meaning it has only one arm on the dial. When you see that, you can ask questions. For example, how certain are you of your life purpose? To what degree are you receiving the full potential of your prosperity path? How aligned are your friends and family to you living your life purpose? How aligned are YOU in living your life purpose? Ask a question, see the number the clock face arm points to as your answer, then reset that arm to zero (well, twelve) so you can ask another question.

My interpretation is that, the higher the number, the more full, robust, or greater the percentage. So a one means low while a twelve means high. And if you started with a twelve and the arm didn't move, your answer is a twelve; in this case, ask the arm to spin around the dial to make sure it's working for you, then ask again to make sure it's a twelve answer. When you get two different numbers that are more than two clicks (or numbers) apart, that means you're working some harmonic balancing in that area. For example, if you ask how satisfied your mother is with your life purpose and then ask how satisfied your family is with your life purpose, and you get two different numbers, you can see there is a 'wobble' in the force around your family and your life purpose.

Another key is that, when you can grow your creation belief to equal your possibility, it calls forward your purpose in a way that's bigger than what you've ever experienced before. Your purpose can lead to exponential results. This is a pivotal moment because it can destabilize your world. For example, you may need to grow in unexpected ways to match your purpose and make the most of your prosperity path. Or you may be guided to touch a million people through your work and, chances are, that won't happen by doing things the way you've always done them. When the world feels chaotic, your purpose contributes vibrantly and robustly to ground the energy into what really matters in the moment. It allows you to realize you are more than capable of what you are being called to do. And you will have the resources you need as you take the first step, then the second, etc.

A major teaching came out of a recent client session, which is that we lose when we chase what is inside from the outside. That is, you cannot chase happiness on the outside because you can only find it inside—and it is not dependent on any external factor. You have the capacity to choose your experience in every moment. What that means for our purposes here is that you can choose your purpose by pursuing opportunities for the experience and know that whatever is not in alignment with your purpose will eventually fall away. Conversely, what is needed to support actualizing your purpose will reveal itself as you stay in action toward it.

You can channel your purpose in different ways. Choose the one that is your truth. For example, someone who is a teacher can teach grade school kids, they can work in a corporate job and educate their colleagues, they can become a motivational speaker, or they can become a business development mentor. There are a lot of ways to channel that truth as a teacher, but it doesn't necessarily have to be the one where they are supervising young kids.

Altogether, when in manifesting mode, there are many truths available in any given moment, depending on your perspective. Choose the one that feels good for you. If your life purpose has led you to be a coal miner up until now but that doesn't feel good, then you wouldn't necessarily claim that as your purpose. However, it may be true that you like to be wandering around in dark places. That could lead you to become an internationally known spelunker that discovers amazing archeological finds below the earth's surface. Take the expanded view of where you are to see new possibilities.

About Friends and Family

We need to digress into considering the one support system most people rely on for making changes—friends and family. Despite what you want to believe, friends and family are not going to necessarily help you or even condone you in breaking out and living your prosperity path. It's usually unconscious behavior or thinking on their part. Here's why you can't rely on friends and family the way you might like to believe is possible.

They know you as they always have...you 'live' in a box in their heads. That means they may not be able to translate who they know and expect you to be into something new. They're usually the last to know when you've changed. You've probably experienced that at different points in your life. Too often, when your personal growth discoveries take you away from established family or relationship patterns with longtime friends, that can be grounds to radically change or even end the relationship. People who have known you for a long time are not going to get it. When you grow, they have to grow with you and they may not be willing or able to do so. While people like change, they don't want to be changed. So you need support from someone outside of your established circle of family and friends to give you objective guidance and perspective.

Also, your transformation or upshift might feel risky to them. Their job is to love you. As a result, they will do whatever they have to do to protect you, including shooting down your dreams or your progress. They will be risk-averse, and they will potentially guide you into not taking what they perceive as risks to live your purpose. So, "Oh, honey, don't do that. You might get hurt there." They're going to want to protect you. That is about them vs. your business growth or success trajectory.

Now, there may be people who fully support your growth and all the changes that come with it, including the changes that affect them. This is a minority of people, but they do exist and should not be dismissed because of the others who hold you back, even when it's unintentional.

Friends and family often can't see your blind spots so they can't see how you have not been living from your purposeful wisdom. They're not objective. Unfortunately, you can't solve a problem with the same energy that created it and they have been part of your creation process. So if your purpose goes away from what they know and expect, they might perceive somehow unconsciously that as a rejection of what they've shared with you. People do what feels best for them, but that can also mean they put themselves before you in their reflection of you, because it's not going to feel good for them to not be there with you. They may just want to reject the changes altogether.

Even more, their vision of your prosperity path comes from what they know, which can be a little prescriptive. "Oh, do it this way." Their suggestion likely has nothing to do with you. And it's limited by what they know in their world and/or with what makes them happy, which is about them—not about you. My client's mother is just waiting for her to move back to Small Town USA and live two blocks down the street from her—meaning they are on two different wavelengths. Family and friends are not typically your ideal target market nor are they knowledgeable about business so, unfortunately, they can't give you meaningful feedback or guidance on your prosperity path. They'll give advice, ideas, and suggestions based on their prescription for success, which is about them—not you.

When you choose to live from your wisdom, it's going to change you. And that will change how they need to relate to you. People like change but they don't want to be changed. When you grow, they have to grow with you (or not), which becomes a potential deterrent for their support of you living and working from your unique prosperity path. Your ability to make a living from your wisdom might cause them to have to look at where they are out of integrity with their own work or career.

Lastly, if they haven't done "the work," you will see their wound, but not necessarily your reflection in the proverbial mirror of their advice. For example, they might think that living and working from your wisdom is a pipe dream, that you should just hunker down and do what you need to do, or that it's a fantasy to live from your wisdom in creating your own economy. They believe there is a certain way to earn money, which is their worldview and has nothing to do with you. Remember that their perspective is not about you but is about their limitation and desire to protect you from their experience. In other words, their life wound is showing.

Micro-Moments of Choice Create Your Path

Every day, you are presented with micro-moments of choice. What you choose in those moments creates your life experience. You can eat the garden salad or the chocolate cake, focus on a job or on building a business, follow your current path or choose one that feels more purposeful; essentially, every choice you make takes you either toward or away from your purposeful path. And your purposeful path is like an internal GPS that leads to prosperity.

You can choose your prosperity path through your own business, as is the focus of this book, or you can work for others as your prosperity path. In some ways, that's easier...you know what's expected of you and how much you will earn from doing it. At the same time, you are trading your life force energy for whatever you choose to do so if it doesn't feel good more often than not, consider now—and now, and now—your micro-moments of choice. You can be / do / have something different, but it requires making new choices.

There will come a time (maybe now) when the pain of changing is less than the pain of staying the same. What you thought impossible will become more attainable. You can either honor that unfolding or you can keep doing what you have been doing, in which case you will likely be invited to choose again and again. Whatever you choose, you are responsible for it. You cannot blame anyone else for your lack of fulfillment on any level because you are choosing it. You have the power of choice and your future in your own hands.

Should you choose to follow a new path, you may have to pursue new activities, gain new insights, and think new thoughts. This choice will have consequences. You will be outgrowing your current circumstances, which could include outgrowing relationships, beliefs, environment, habits, etc. The familiar will pull you away from that newly unfolding path. At that point, it would be easier to succumb to what worked up until now—only it will no longer work in the same way. In the extreme, you can change or become obsolete . . . but only you can make that choice because you have to live with it.

As you grow in your conscious awareness, your logical mind will struggle with what to do because it wants to express your purpose if it makes sense. At the same time, your intuitive wisdom will ask you to do things that defy logic. This means you could experience an inner checkmate, or an impasse, that will create pressure. At that point, you will either break down or break through to your next best level.

The power of life is constant, relentless, and dynamic creation arising with each moment. You encounter these moments over and over again throughout each day. You make choices just as frequently. In this micro-moment of choice, you can adopt what you've learned through this book to live in alignment with your purposeful prosperity path, to follow what is shifting and emerging within you, to defy the logic of the life you've built until now . . . or stay in the comfort zone of your current circumstances. Neither is wrong! But you will live differently depending on your choice. And you will be free to make another new choice in the future so you can't get it wrong.

One helpful hint is to mentally project forward and feel how it would be to *not* make a change by identifying the potential regrets from not trying something new and more aligned with your purposeful prosperity. And there may not be any! Or you could feel into the fears and obstacles either way—to change or not to change—to determine whether they are real enough to stop you. Remember that things are shifting in this very micro-moment, so this is not the time to 'go through the motions' or do what you've always done. Instead, this is about engaging with your essential energy to crystallize your life compass, your inner GPS, toward your purpose and prosperity path. Feel what is 'right,' meaning centered in your intuitive right brain, as a guide for what is emotionally and energetically oriented toward your next best level.

As you develop perception, you're developing natural discernment about what is aligned for you and how to express purpose through everything you do. Innately, as you grow, you are naturally living more deeply into your purpose every day, every hour, every minute.

Additionally, you are a source of energy personified, meaning that you can call on and access the power of your purpose in every situation. You can discern your next steps on command. If the way is not clear, you can wait for clarity—and waiting is not a passive activity. A lot happens when you're waiting—you have time to prepare, finish loose ends, build your new business launch pad, and more. Your purpose honors who you are and gives you voice, strength, and resilience.

Hopefully this helps you know what to expect, how to facilitate growing your awareness, and what you can do to continue claiming your right prosperity path. It's a process. As you live and work both the energy and the practicalities of your next-level success, "stuff" is going to come up. The good news is that each of those circumstances are signs that you are going beyond your comfort zone to walk your purposeful prosperity path for success.

Investing in awareness, insight derived from that awareness, and your personal wisdom will pay off in terms of clarity, life satisfaction, and internal balance—which is true prosperity.

Summary

Transformative learning is defined as an educational process that leads to reevaluating life so far, revealing the gems of what people intrinsically know as a result of being 'seasoned' by life. I feel that's one of my personal sweet spots because I'm here to support actualizing potential through transformation, then—ideally—pulling that through a profitable business that delivers value. Thank you for allowing me to live my purpose through this book. I trust it has at least initiated a new level of success and prosperity for you through expanded perspective.

So much about purpose and prosperity is what we're willing to allow and how we want to achieve our desires. And the only person who can determine what feels good and right about that for you is you. Even Maslow, the father of psychological insight (aka, Maslow's Hierarchy), says it's a rare and difficult achievement to know what we want.

The pay-off is that knowing your purpose can support your self-affinity, or self-esteem, despite external judgments, projections of other people, and experiences. The process of discovering your purpose offers the potential to restore faith and dignity and assures your place in the world. No conformist ever made history and, yet, we are conditioned to seek belonging as a survival mechanism. To be successful on your prosperity path may mean doing something different than anyone else has ever tried, which requires that inner fortitude which can be bolstered through knowing your purpose.

When you begin to find and become yourself, when you notice how you are already found within by being who you were born to be, you also discover other stuff, like other people's perceptions and your striving to get more of the things you think will make you happy. The issue becomes how to stop being who you are not, how to release false obligations from trying to please others and gain affection, to power-grab for a sense of security, or to break the constraints of psychic constrictions that keep you small and contained. It's about breaking out of limbo, indecision, disappointments, old stories, potential humiliation, addiction to what keeps you numb and distracted, letting go of those you thought you couldn't live without because they hold you back by who they think you are . . . and by enduring the illumination of your purposeful truth.

And that is the point of all mastery teachings . . . to feed yourself with what makes you come alive and then share it with others. In my world, there is a way to do that and allow it to become your prosperity path. Being a business owner is not necessarily for everyone but it is the fastest way to surface who you are and the value your unique perspective and experience has in the world.

Sooner or later, I believe each of us has the compelling urge to break through the status quo, to discover our unique path to freedom, and then enjoy living it full out. When you have heard the calling of what's meant for you in living your purpose and crafting your prosperity path, it will compel you to follow it. May this book be helpful to you in doing so.

My Gift to You #1

I have a video that is a mini-class on how to identify your ideal clients. In it, I cover more than what most people do in several sessions—and it's my gift to you!

Why? Because the information does the world no good if it's only sitting in my mind. I WANT you to have this information so you can help more people and enjoy prosperity as you do.

Here is a quick list of what is covered:

- Intangible products
- A note on niches
- The conversation happening in your potential client's mind
- Questions to define your niche
- How to evaluate your niche
- Marketing funnels
- Your Unique Selling Proposition (USP)
- Principles to attract your ideal clients

As you can see, I don't believe in holding anything back. :+)
Go to this page to watch—no optin or obligation required:

lynnscheurell.com/identify-ideal-clients/

May this resource help you go further on your prosperity path! And please feel free to drop me a line to let me know what you got from it! :+)

My Gift to You #2

I have an email series that provides an overview of the GEENI for Change system. It covers the five keys to the system and how you can use them for yourself starting immediately.

Why do I give this away for free? Because I want you (and everyone!) to know how to use the resources you already have to help you make more informed decisions.

You will learn how to (re)claim your personal power through insight, the keys to discerning the right answers for you, and ways to expand or get fresh perspective on your current circumstances. It's about understanding where you are now and what it is showing you to leverage it to new results. When you do that, you've met your personal GEENI for Change.

Go to this page to get your free e-course now (and, obviously, it asks for your email address so you can receive it in your inbox):

lynnscheurell.com/geeni/

My wish for you is that this be a tool you can use for the rest of your days on your prosperity path and more.

My Gift to You #3

There were a number of exercises in this book that might be helpful to work through on paper. I put those together for you in this downloadable PDF so it's easy for you to work with the exercises, think about what you really want, and plan your next action steps.

This companion PDF includes such exercises as:

- Questions to Ask Yourself
- Your Life Purpose Formula
- Your Prime Directive
- The Real Value of Your Time
- Your Prosperity Path Worksheet

Go to this page to get your free downloadable PDF (note: I do ask for your email in case I can share future insights relevant to your purposeful prosperity path):

lynnscheurell.com/prosperity-exercises/

My wish for you is this be a tool you can use for the rest of your days in discovering and working your next level on your prosperity path.

About the Author

Lynn Scheurell is a professional catalyst, intuitive, and best-selling author. As an authority on translating nebulous and/or complex concepts to clear, concise language, she effectively communicates life-changing ideas with clarity.

Since 1998, she has worked with thousands of business owners, life-mastery students, and visionary leaders around the world to discover their unique essence to deliver it through their businesses, books, and presentations. She teaches why you're getting the results you are getting now as well as how to manifest the results you want through intentional clarity.

By definition, a catalyst provokes significant change; this is what people expect in working with Lynn. She is an innovator and facilitator of the complex made simple. Concurrently, Lynn also knows the proven keys to business success in systems, marketing, and strategic action. She has developed her innovation and brainstorming skills, lateral systems thinking capabilities, and high sensitivity to unseen energies that can be utilized to optimize flow and intentional results.

Focusing on writing several books, she currently resides in Oro Valley, Arizona. She considers herself to be a practical visionary, idea generator and facilitator of positive transformation through clarity consciousness.

Lynn can be reached at her personal website at: **LynnScheurell.com**.

Twitter: **Twitter.com/LynnScheurell**

Facebook: **Facebook.com/MyCreativeCatalyst**

LinkedIn: **Linkedin.com/in/lynnscheurell/**

Other Books
by Lynn Scheurell

You've Arrived!: A 5-Step System to Bypass Your Logical Mind, Activate Your Intuitive Potential and Gain Perfect Clarity For Your Business

Feng Shui for Entrepreneurs: Harnessing the Power of Your Environment for Business Success

Perspectives: Digital Transformation Through the Lens of Strategic Marketing

The Energy of Money: Understanding Your Money Messages: Discover How the Universe is Talking to You